SHHHH...LISTEN!

PRACTICAL PARENTING STEPS TO GET YOUR KIDS TO LISTEN THAT WORK! AGE 3-8

SIENNA NEEL

This book is dedicated to my Mother

*Who divided her love amongst six children and each child
still had all her love*

Ram.P

CONTENTS

Sienna Neel

Dear Reader, Thank You for chosing my book ... after all

... who is the writer without their readers? a question i have often asked. I do not have the answer, but it gives me great joy to know that by sharing my knowledge i have improved someone's life, given them hope or just helped guide in the right direction. So as a token of gratitude, i share a little gift ...

i really appreciate it !

ENJOY A FREE GIFTCARD ON ME !

SCAN HERE TO CLAIM*

*Currently only available to US and UK residents.   *Terms & Conditions Apply

INTRODUCTION

"Raising children is a creative endeavor, an art rather than a science."

— *BRUNO BETTELHEIM*

We've all heard that classic parental phrase for when we want to get our kids to do something: "Because I said so." Maybe we've even used it ourselves a few times. After all, we're the parents, so we rely on that level of authority. But if you think back to when you were a kid, you'll probably remember that "because I said so" wasn't exactly the most compelling argument. Instead of following along with a parent's advice, kids who hear it are more likely to resist the advice, all because of the poor communication inherent in the phrase.

Whether you're a new parent feeling out of your comfort zone, someone who wants to have a less volatile relationship between yourself and your child, or an educator who's having trouble getting some of the kids in your class to behave, improving your communication skills for talking with kids can significantly improve kids' behavioral issues and your relationship with them.

You know how difficult it can be to get your child to listen to you sometimes. They might be perfect angels one day, saying "please" and "thank you" and cleaning up after play-time, and the next they seem like completely different people, stubborn and prone to tantrums. You want what's best for your child, and you understand things about the world that they might not yet know themselves, so you try to guide them in the right direction. However, when you are unable to properly communicate with your child, this advice can lead to an argument and frequently ends in tears—possibly for both of you. The whole ordeal can leave you feeling uncertain about the relationship between yourself and your child, and even questioning your parenting skills.

The good news is that any adult can learn how to improve their communication with kids. With better knowledge of child psychology and the importance of clear communication, you can talk to your child in a way that helps them understand their own feelings and your wishes and goals for them. In this book, you'll learn about the way your child thinks, how kids process emotions, and what you can do to speak to them in a way they'll understand. You'll also learn strategies for fostering better communication skills for both yourself and your child.

Child development can be intimidating. You might worry that your child isn't getting the tools they need to grow and learn properly, especially if there is trouble communicating. But with a little help, you can ensure your child is well on his or her way to a healthy, happy life.

Child development includes multiple milestones that kids reach at their own pace. In the phase of early childhood, which lasts from birth to about eight years old, your child goes through the most development in the shortest amount of time. They learn to walk and talk—and that means communication skills. As your child begins school and forms friendships with classmates, they'll learn more about the world around them. Communication skills become very important during this period, as your child will want to ask questions and form bonds with others. Practicing good communication at home can significantly improve their ability to communicate with peers and teachers in an honest and clear way.

I am a personal life coach who has been working with kids for more than 10 years. I have helped many parents learn the principles for communicating effectively with their kids— and have helped just as many kids develop the communication skills they'll need for the rest of their lives. In my studies of child behavioral psychology, I have learned and instilled the socialization methods necessary to encourage healthy child development. With this book, I hope to help you understand and practice these methods in order to improve your relationship with your child, and your child to listen.

Establishing healthy communication with your child can significantly improve the parent-child relationship. When disagreements arise, they will no longer be the source of anger and tears; instead, they will be opportunities for your child to learn and for you to guide them through the often-confusing world around them. Your child will listen to you not because they feel they have to, but because they understand why you're telling them they can or can't do something. This creates a healthier bond between the two of you, one based on trust and honesty.

By improving your communication skills and those of your child, you ensure your child is receiving the developmental guidance they need as they grow up. As they move on to middle childhood and adolescence, they will be equipped with the tools they need to understand and convey their emotions to their peers. Healthy communication skills early on in life allow them to continue to thrive and maintain a positive relationship with you for years to come.

1

WHY UNDERSTANDING CHILD PSYCHOLOGY IS IMPORTANT

We often think of kids as just smaller versions of ourselves. We might assume they think the same way we do, but in actuality this is far from the truth. Kids are still developing, so their minds work very differently from our own. They haven't experienced all of the socialization and growth that we have, so they can have trouble grasping certain concepts or worldviews. Kids also take in and process information differently than we do. This causes a lot of frustration when it comes to getting kids to listen.

Often, the problem isn't a purposefully stubborn or disobedient child. Instead, the root of the issue is that we don't account for how a child processes what we tell them. Recognizing that child psychology is separate from adult psychology is the first step in addressing communication issues.

The idea that kids think differently than we do wasn't extensively embraced until the early 1930s. The person most responsible for changing how we think about childhood development was the Swiss psychologist Jean Piaget, who theorized that kids actually experience the world differently than adults. When he heard this theory, Albert Einstein reportedly said the discovery was "so simple that only a genius could have thought of it" (Cherry, 2019, para. 2). It might not be something we assume immediately, but when we start thinking of kids in this new light, many of their behaviors start to make a lot more sense. This is the basis of child psychology.

By accounting for developmental differences, we can forge a closer bond with our kids because we're able to meet them on their level. We can explain things in ways that make sense to them, and in turn can find it easier to understand their perspective. For parents and all other caretakers, having a better idea of how kids develop and perceive the world allows us to speak and listen more effectively.

FACTORS THAT IMPACT CHILD PSYCHOLOGY

Childhood development is influenced by a number of different internal and external factors. You have probably heard of the old "nature vs. nurture" debate, which aims to determine whether our personalities are a product of genetics or their environment.

Psychologists tend to agree on a midway point between the two extremes. Kids can be influenced both by their nature *and* the way they are nurtured. However, more weight is usually given to the impact of the "nurture" side of the equation, in part because we can change it.

When discussing child psychology, internal factors that influence child psychology can be defined as anything a child was born with innately. Typically, this means characteristics determined solely by genetics. These factors and their impact on child development are difficult if not impossible to change because they are instinctual. There is very little anyone can do to change our child's genes once they are born.

External factors, on the other hand, impact your child's personality after birth. It is easier to recognize how factors like socialization and family life might influence how your child sees the world. Just as a certain experience might help us see life in a different light, so too can our kids. In fact, kids are often even more affected by their experiences and environments than adults because kids are still developing.

In child psychology, there are three major contexts that are recognized as having a significant impact on development: cultural, social, and socioeconomic.

Cultural Context

Culture consists of the unique behaviors, activities, and lifestyles in a certain population. We tend not to notice these traits in our own culture because we are so used to it. However, if we travel to other countries or states, we often find that our cultural norms are different or nonexistent there. It can be very hard to immerse ourselves fully in a new culture once we're adults, whether it's a vacation or a permanent move, simply because we are so accustomed to our own.

Culture can vary significantly from region to region, and what's normal in one culture may be abnormal or even frowned upon by another. For example, in some cultures giving a thumbs up signifies that the recipient did well, while in others it's actually a rude gesture. Food, art, and education also vary widely.

Common discipline methods for kids can differ too. Each of these differences has an impact on the kids that grow up in these cultures. The way kids relate to their parents, the type of child care we provide, and the education they get at school and at home are all products of our culture, so it's important to recognize what kind of lessons our culture teaches our still-developing kids.

Societal Influences and Expectations

The way kids are socialized has a powerful effect on personality and disposition. Forming healthy relationships with family and friends is an essential part of this process. Kids who don't spend a lot of time around their peers may struggle to practice their communication skills, often falling behind and having trouble identifying and expressing emotions. They may also have difficulty managing conflict if they haven't built up these skills, or if they are surrounded by examples of poor conflict management like arguing and physical violence. Kids often internalize the behaviors they see as well as the ones they experience firsthand. Providing your child with positive examples of healthy relationships and assisting them as they begin interacting with other kids and teachers helps them develop good communication skills and healthy relationships of their own.

Socioeconomic Factors

Socioeconomic factors include a family's social class, their financial situation, their jobs, where they live, and the education options that are available.

Each of these three factors plays an important role in child development. For example, if a family doesn't have much money and lives somewhere with poor public education, their child may struggle more than their more well-off peers. They may not be able to address any educational gaps at home if their parents or caretakers work long hours. Further issues may arise if kids lack access to sufficient nutrition and health care.

Of course, parents can raise a happy, healthy child even if they aren't rich. While kids who grow up in low-income households may have fewer opportunities than some of their peers, positive experiences with social and cultural contexts can help make up the difference. Still, it's important to account for the influence of socioeconomic status in child development. When you recognize how these factors come into play, you will better understand the needs of your child and what you can do to help fulfill those needs.

AREAS OF CHILD DEVELOPMENT

Now that you know the different contexts that influence child psychology, you can see how they contribute to child development. The three main areas of child development are physical, cognitive, and emotional. A healthy child should develop in each of these areas. Keeping an eye on your own child's physical, cognitive, and emotional skills can help ensure they're getting everything they need for regular development in each area.

In order to know if your child's development is on track, you must first know what's expected of them at each stage and area of child development. Let's take a look at the different areas now.

Physical

Your child's physical development typically follows a predictable series of events. Babies will learn to pick their heads up and roll over, and as your child progresses into the toddler stage they will begin to crawl, walk, and run with confidence and less risk of overbalancing and falling over.

Most kids learn to walk between one and two years old, so by the time your child is three or older, they should have relative mastery over these basic movements, barring any health conditions that might delay their physical development.

In some cases, issues with physical development can point to future troubles in cognitive and emotional development. Some kids are simply slower walkers than others, but occasionally these issues are more serious than your child simply being a late bloomer. If you notice significant delays in your child's physical abilities, speak to their doctor about possible causes and how this might impact other areas of development.

Cognitive

Cognitive development refers to the way your child thinks and perceives the world around them. Even as babies, kids generally show interest in their environment—for example, a baby might watch the spinning mobile above their head and follow its movements with their eyes. As kids continue to grow older, their cognitive abilities improve. They'll start to retain information, whether through something taught to them or something learned through experience. They'll also start using their imagination, problem-solving, and critical-thinking skills. These are important skills for communication and conflict resolution, as they allow kids to understand what they're being told and decide how they're going to react to that information.

Emotional

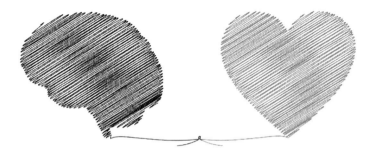

A child's emotional development is how well they are able to feel, recognize, and display their emotions. The older your child gets, the more complex these emotions will be, and the more trouble they may have understanding them. Simple emotions like anger and happiness are fairly easy to grasp and express, but complex ones like guilt and confidence may prove to be more confusing. You can assist in this process by encouraging your child to be honest and open about their emotions. Let them attempt to explain how they feel, and try not to discredit these emotions, even when they may not be appropriate for the situation. Through understanding their own feelings, kids are better able to regulate emotional expression as they grow up. They also get better at recognizing others' emotions and reacting to them accordingly. For example, a child with a high level of emotional development might see another child who is upset and try to comfort them. This showcases their ability to not only realize the signs of sadness but practice compassion and understanding.

Emotional development is closely related to a child's social skills. The more emotionally mature your child is, the better they will handle interpersonal conflicts. It can be tough for some kids to learn to understand,regulate, and appropriately manage their emotions. It's common for young kids to get upset to the point of tears at the idea of sharing their toys or playing the game someone else wants to play. However, practicing these skills through various forms of social interaction will teach them how to compromise, share, and collaborate to make and maintain relationships. A lack of adequate socialization can lead to problems with a child's emotional development. With good examples of healthy relationships and enough opportunities to socialize, kids will have an easier time grasping concepts like friendship, trust, and respect for authority figures like parents and teachers.

WHY UNDERSTANDING CHILD PSYCHOLOGY IS IMPORTANT

Understanding the psychology that influences your child's actions can help you be a better parent, guardian, or educator. By understanding your child's needs, you can ensure you're meeting those needs. It also allows you to speak to kids in a way they understand. If you're trying to explain to a toddler why they need to go to bed on time, they probably won't understand if you tell them it's because they need to maintain a good sleep cycle for healthy brain function.

Breaking this information down into something they can more easily understand will help you convince them to respect bedtime rules. For example, you might tell them that if they go to bed now, they'll have more energy to play with their friends tomorrow. This is something they can understand that will motivate them to follow your rules. Child psychology can also help you recognize reasons why your child might act differently than others. If they have different cultural or socioeconomic contexts, they might lack some of the opportunities other kids get and therefore could develop more slowly. By recognizing your child's unique needs, you can address them more appropriately and effectively.

Of course, it is always possible that your child is an outlier and doesn't follow some of the expected behavior and development timelines. This isn't necessarily a bad thing; the common knowledge we have about when and how kids develop is based on averages, which means there are as many kids who advance quicker than there are who advance slower. Recognizing these averages simply provides a frame of reference to help better understand our kids. If we notice that their development in a certain area is falling behind those averages, we can better identify contributing factors. This allows us to account for potential difficulties and focus on improving these underdeveloped areas.

Understanding child psychology also gives you a better idea of your child's perspective on issues. An outburst may seem completely random and unprovoked, but it might make more sense when you consider how your child's psychology differs from your own. They might lack the ability to regulate their emotions the same way adults do, so anything that makes them feel a little upset could potentially lead to an outburst. When you understand where your child is coming from and why they might be reacting the way they are, it's easier to push aside the frustration you might feel at the outburst and resolve the issue.

Finally, having a basic grasp of child psychology will help you set reasonable behavioral expectations and rules. Without it, you might establish rules that your child has no hope of following at their current developmental stage. For example, if your child's memory is still developing, it might be unfair to expect them to remember to follow rules you haven't mentioned to them in a while. If you account for this possibility, you can make sure to remind them of the rule when it becomes relevant again, and you can temper your frustration if they forget and the rule gets broken. Less anger leads to better communication and helps your kids correct their mistakes without feeling afraid or hurt by your reaction.

How to Better Understand Your Child

You can use child psychology to improve your understanding of your child's wants and needs. By giving your child the tools they need to develop and address any issues when they arise, you set the stage for better understanding between the two of you and better communication. Here are a few tips for getting to know your child and the way they think, feel, and react to their surroundings.

Spend Quality Time Together

One of the most reliable ways to encourage development and bond with your child is to simply spend time with them. If you often find yourself busy with work or other activities that separate you from your child, try to make a concerted effort to block off time for them. Ask them questions about their day and let them talk about what interests them. You can support this by asking specific questions that invite them to give a more detailed answer. Instead of simply asking if they had a good day, you might ask them what kind of games they played with their friends or the drawing they made. This kind of language invites kids to open up and show enthusiasm for what they like and dislike, which can give you more insight into who your child is as a person and the best strategies for communication. Avoid making judgments about your child's fears and insecurities, as kids are especially susceptible to discouragement at this point in their development. Even if you don't mean to, laughing at or brushing off a source of fear could cause them to feel embarrassed, and next time they might not feel comfortable discussing their fears with you.

Pay Attention to Environmental Factors

Another good method for understanding your child is to pay attention to their environment. Consider their home life, school, and any extracurricular programs or clubs they might be part of. Watch out for any potential negative influences, like arguments at home or community disputes that your child might pick up on. Even though you might assume these kinds of things would go right over your child's head, kids are often more perceptive (not to mention impressionable) than we believe. Identifying these negative influences could help explain why your child is having issues with aggression or shyness.

The more time you spend with your child and the more attention you are able to give them, the deeper the parent-child bond will become. Paying attention to their development—and understanding its psychological underpinnings—will help you lay the foundation for good communication.

2

BECOME THE MASTER OF YOUR EMOTIONS

I t's important to understand your child's mind, but it's also important to understand your own mind. As the old adage goes, communication is a two-way street. If you want your child to listen to you, you have to be willing to listen to them, and you also need to know how to communicate effectively. One of the biggest roadblocks for communication between kids and parents is anger.

Anger can turn a productive discussion into an argument that helps no one. When we get angry, we get defensive, and we become worse at explaining our point of view. Instead, we start trying to 'win' the argument. But when we're talking to our kids, there should be no winners or losers. We are just trying to get them to understand what we want them to do, not to debate them. If we resort to yelling and lose control of ourselves, we tend to resort to the dreaded "because I said so." Our kids may also be less likely to listen to us because they get defensive at our raised tone of voice, just like we would get defensive if someone yelled at us. They stop listening to what we're saying, and we stop saying much more than "listen to me or else."

Needless to say, this isn't any way to hold a productive conversation. If we want our kids to listen, we have to learn to control our anger when we talk to them. We can't get so wrapped up in the "argument" that we end up in a screaming match with our own kids, and we definitely don't want to say anything cruel that we'll regret later. In order to communicate with our kids, we need to learn to recognize sources of our own anger, readjust our thinking, and develop practices for calming us down when we feel we're on the verge of screaming. Deescalating the conversation lets you more effectively convince your child to listen, and it helps you better manage any tantrums your child may throw during the discussion.

ANGER TRIGGERS

Anger is a strong emotion that we tend to express before we even recognize we're feeling it. It can bubble up inside us quickly, causing us to say things we don't mean just because we're lashing out at someone. While it can be hard to stop ourselves from reacting in anger in the heat of the moment, we can make it easier for ourselves by learning to recognize our anger triggers. If we can anticipate when we'll feel angry, we can address these potential issues and calm down more effectively.

Anger triggers are the experiences, activities, and phrases that are most likely to make us angry. We encounter many different anger triggers throughout the day. These might include general things like getting stuck in traffic or speaking to a rude customer or coworker at your job. These kinds of triggers are likely to make anyone angry. There are also more specific anger triggers that reflect your personal pet peeves and insecurities. For example, if you're someone who has trouble feeling listened to in your life, you might get more upset at getting talked over than someone who hasn't had the same experiences. Our individual anger triggers can come from our lifestyles, our previous experiences, and even past traumas. However, just because these events are capable of making us angry doesn't mean we have to give in to that anger. If we learn to recognize and anticipate our anger when we come into contact with anger triggers, we can regain control over ourselves and calm down much faster than if these triggers catch us off guard.

Common Anger Triggers for Parents

As parents, there are many behaviors our kids can engage in that might make us angry. We love our kids, but that doesn't mean they can never upset us. We might feel frustrated when they don't listen, upset when they're not doing well at school, or hurt if they attack us.

Some of the behaviors our kids do that commonly lead to anger include talking back, whining, crying, yelling, bickering with friends or siblings, having a meltdown, and acting stubborn. These behaviors are more likely to make us mad if we're already in a stressful situation, such as running late to an important event, or dealing with their fussy siblings. We can also feel a sort of protective rage if someone hurts or upsets our kids, and we may inadvertently project some of this anger onto the child. For example, if our child nearly has a dangerous accident, we might turn our anger on them rather than the person or object that would have hurt them. While we may only be reacting this way because we care about their safety, all the child sees is our anger.

Being a parent is a stressful job, and it's one that comes with many upsides but also plenty of aggravation. The previously discussed examples are all common triggers for anger, and it's natural to feel this way when these events occur. But just because the feelings themselves are understandable doesn't mean that it's acceptable to express these feelings by yelling or retaliating. In order to shift how we express our anger as parents, we must first understand why these triggers make us so angry.

. . .

How to React to These Triggers

Reframing the way we think about and understand our anger can help us manage it. One of the biggest underlying causes of anger in parents is a sense of inadequacy. We want to be the best parents we can be, and when our kids act out or don't excel in school and relationships, we may take this as a sign that we have failed as parents. To be sure, parenting is tough, especially if you are a first-time parent. We're often not entirely sure what the best way to raise our kids is, and because of this, we can feel inadequate and defensive if we start thinking we're parenting them wrong. Oftentimes, "Feelings of inadequacy occur when we are jarred out of preconceived notions of what kids need, what they should be like, or how they ought to respond to us" (Stosny, 2015, para. 5). If our child acts differently than we would expect them to—ie, in a way that doesn't align with our ideas of how a well-adjusted, healthy child should act—we tend to take this as a referendum on our parenting skills. It can make us feel vulnerable, which activates the fight-or-flight response and, in some cases, full-blown anger.

Feelings of inadequacy tend to morph into anger when we stop seeing our kids as individuals and instead focus on how they "should be" acting. Each child has his or her own individual needs and personality. As parents, it's our job to adapt our parenting style to suit these needs, and to gently encourage our kids to grow and develop into happy, healthy adults.

If your child is acting out and you feel yourself getting angry, consider whether the anger is really warranted or whether you're really just feeling defensive about your parenting. To be sure, there are some behaviors from kids that are unacceptable, but trying to correct these behaviors by getting angry at your child isn't a productive way to go about it. You can always adjust your parenting style until you find one that works well for you and your child. Take time to listen to what your child needs, and take a moment to calm yourself down before you address your child's anger.

HANDLING TANTRUMS WITHOUT ANGER

When kids throw tantrums, our initial response is often aggravation. Maybe we're somewhere public, and the last thing we want is for our child to have a meltdown in the middle of the grocery store, or a place where they're supposed to be quiet. Maybe we're rushing around and we know stopping and addressing the issue is only going to make us even later than we already are. Maybe we've had a long day at work, we're exhausted, and we just want to relax, so our child's outburst feels like just one more annoyance on the ever-growing pile.

Whatever we might have been doing before the tantrum began, that characteristic wailing and stomping is never a good sign. It's a huge source of stress, and if we're around other people when it happens, we might fear being judged. Taken altogether, it's no wonder we tend to get angry when our kids throw tantrums.

Frustration might be understandable, but that doesn't mean it's the best response. When we're stressed and tense, our kids are too. When we're terse with them, they notice. This can trigger a meltdown, or make it harder to stop one once it's already in progress. Rather than de-escalating the situation, we might unthinkingly make things worse by raising our voices and punishing kids for their tantrums. This doesn't teach our kids emotional management skills, nor does it help us manage the conflict. The best way to handle a temper tantrum is to first calm yourself down, and then calm your child down. In order to do this, it helps to have a better understanding of why your child is throwing a tantrum in the first place and what you can do to handle it in a level-headed way.

Why Kids Throw Tantrums

While you may know some adults who seem to have mood swings as uncontrollable as kids do, temper tantrums are much more common in young kids. As adults, we have the vocabulary necessary to express our emotions with our words. We also have years of practicing the emotional maturity skills necessary for proper communication. Whether your emotional maturity is top-notch or a little rusty, you have still gone through all the mental development necessary to regulate your emotions. However, kids have not. As we discussed in the previous chapter, kids are still undergoing a lot of mental development at this stage, including the parts of their brains that help them manage their emotions. Because of this, they tend to be more prone to angry outbursts and tears when there's a conflict or disturbance to their routine.

It can be hard for us to understand why kids throw tantrums, especially when we're thinking about them like tiny adults. We watch our kids ball up their fists and start crying after their favorite show ends and we think, "Why are they so upset? Don't they know it's not such a big deal?" Of course, the problem is that kids don't know this. They often don't understand that these issues, which seem major in their minds, are very minor in the grand scheme of life because they haven't had the life experiences to tell them that. Their life is only what they have experienced so far, so something as small as the wrong show playing on TV is a big deal. On top of this, kids lack the language needed to communicate their distress in any other way. They often resort to crying, yelling, throwing, or hitting because these are the only ways they know to make an impact on the world around them. This kind of behavior is more likely to continue if we reaffirm this belief. If, however, we give them tools to express themselves another way, and we don't let the volume of their voice dictate our response to their tantrum, we can encourage our kids to handle their anger more appropriately.

When we understand that kids throw tantrums because they lack the knowledge and skill to express themselves the way adults might—not because they're being spiteful or want to be a problem—we're better at keeping our anger out of the picture. We can be reasonable in our approach to our kids' anger without adding our own anger to the mix. Instead of getting mad at our kids for acting out, we see the situation as an opportunity to prevent future tantrums. This level-headed approach keeps us from escalating the tantrum or saying something that could at best upset our kids further, and at worst stick with them long after the tantrum. We must recognize that while tantrums aren't completely unavoidable, especially in early childhood, we can still help our kids get a handle on their emotions and teach them how to process these feelings early on in life.

Our goal during a tantrum should be not just to get our kids to stop crying but to help them learn to calm themselves. We must teach kids the best way to express their sadness and anger, and we must encourage them to use their words to explain how they feel rather than jumping right to a melt-down. Through this, we will expand their emotional maturity and ensure future meltdowns are more manageable.

Why You Should Stay Calm

Kids often learn more from us than we think. They listen, watch, and emulate what we say and do. They can pick up on cues in our behavior that they then internalize and practice themselves, even if it's a behavior we'd rather they avoid. We can be a positive influence on our kids just as easily as a negative influence. If we practice kindness, compassion, and good listening skills, our kids will pick up on these. If our kids watch us share our possessions with family and neighbors, they become better at sharing with their friends. If they see us at our jobs, they might pretend to work too, even if their understanding of what we actually do at work is a little skewed.

In many cases, we pass along good lessons to our kids this way, or at least get a lighthearted chuckle out of their attempts to play pretend. But we can pass along bad behaviors in the same way. If our kids see and hear us argue with our spouse, they learn all the mean things people say to each other when they're mad. They internalize the idea that it's okay to shout and slam things when we're mad if they see us do it first. The concept of "do as I say, not as I do" doesn't really exist for kids. No matter what we tell them to do, if we don't practice what we preach, they're not going to fully get it.

Nowhere is it more important to practice good values than when we are interacting directly with our kids. When we are face to face with our kids, they pick up even more about our body language and tone. If we sound stressed and angry, they'll subconsciously pick up on these cues and become stressed and angry themselves. Their minds tell them there is something to get upset about, so they do, even if they otherwise wouldn't have escalated the tantrum.

If instead we take a moment to calm ourselves down, they'll pick up on that. They will understand there's nothing to fear in their current situation, and they will stop working themselves up as soon as we show them it's okay to be calm. Once they've internalized your lack of anger, they can let their own anger go, at which point you can ask them to express how they're feeling with their words.

Remaining calm also sets a good example for our kids. If we can stay level-headed in the face of a source of stress, they will copy that behavior, and they'll start to manage sources of stress in their own life in the same way. If we show them that anger or even violence are acceptable solutions, they'll copy these behaviors instead. We want to set the best example we can for our kids, so we should always try to act how we would want them to act. By taking a minute to cool off and talking about our emotions openly with them, they learn that it is okay to do the same thing, whether they're upset with us, another family member, or one of their friends.

How to Calmly Handle Tantrums

You now know why it's so important to stay calm, but it can still be hard to actually put this into practice. We are only human, after all, and it can be hard for us to not leap imme-diately to frustration when our kids do things that upset us. In the middle of a temper tantrum, it's easy to lose our cool and end up acting exactly how we know we shouldn't. In order to stay calm during tantrums, here are a few steps you can follow to address the issue appropriately and some tips for redirecting your anger in a way that won't interfere with your ability to have a conversation with your child.

Take a Breather

Breathing is an invaluable tool for managing anger. When we purposefully calm our breathing, we can back away from the angry feelings stewing inside us and reaffirm control over them. Simple breathing exercises may not seem like much, but they're surprisingly effective. Our breathing rate is connected to our heart beat, our blood pressure, and even our natural response to stress. When we hyperventilate by taking too many quick, shallow breaths, we work ourselves up. By slowing our breathing, we return our pulse and blood pressure to normal, which takes us out of fight or flight mode and helps us deal with problems more effectively.

When you catch yourself getting upset, try not to react right away. Delay the reaction by counting backward from 10 in your head. The time it takes you to get to "one" is enough time for you to reevaluate your response. If you still feel out of balance, take some slow, deep breaths—in through your nose and out through your mouth. Feel the way the air enters and exits your body, and imagine your stress leeching away with each breath. Breathe in and out in steady, even counts until you feel you can manage your anger.

. . .

Listen—Even if You Disagree

Discussions tend to turn into arguments when we don't listen to what the other person is saying. This is as true for conversations with our kids as it is for conversations with other adults.

Failing to listen to your child will only make their tantrum worse, which only increases your headache. If kids feel like you're belittling their feelings, making fun of them, or punishing them for feeling a certain way rather than correcting how they express that feeling, they might be more reluctant to talk to you about their emotions in the future. If they feel like you're talking over them, they can start to yell louder just so they feel like they're heard. In order to communicate with your child, you must listen to them and try to understand why they feel the way they do. This lets them feel like their feelings are validated, which can help them return to a calmer state.

Of course, this doesn't mean you have to agree with them, nor does it mean you should never correct behavior that goes too far. If your child hits you or someone else, if they continue to raise their voice, or if they destroy property, you still need to tell them that what they did was wrong. If they refuse to go to bed even though it's bedtime, it's still important for your child to obey the rules. You shouldn't feel the need to abolish bedtime just because you want to show your child you're listening.

However, you should at least listen to their points of view before determining the best course of action. If the kids don't want to go to bed, ask them why. Maybe they have an activity they want to do, or maybe they aren't sleepy because they're stressed out about something happening tomorrow. Once they start talking to you instead of yelling, and once you've heard what they have to say, you can reward this behavior and come up with an offer that helps them feel heard while sticking to your rules. For example, maybe you could remind them that if they clean their room, they can do that fun activity they wanted to do in the morning. Or, the sooner they get their homework done, the sooner they get to play video games. If they're dreading something tomorrow, ask them why they're worried and how you can help. This shows your child you're listening and willing to compromise. You are still the one in charge, but your child gets rewarded for talking to you about their problems instead of having a meltdown.

Teach Coping Mechanisms

While tantrums are never something we would actively encourage, they do make for great teaching moments. When your child's emotions get the best of them, and when your emotions threaten to do the same, you have an opportunity to change this pattern of behavior for you both. Teach your child how to cope with their emotions so they are less to throw a tantrum in the future.

The kind of coping mechanism that works best for you or your child will vary. Some people respond very well to taking deep breaths. Practicing meditation can also help when you feel emotionally conflicted. Others find that a calming activity like reading or drawing can help them let go of their residual agitation.

Sometimes coping mechanisms can be more physical in nature. For example, you could ask your child to do five jumping jacks when they feel themselves getting angry. This helps them burn off excess energy while bringing a bit of fun to the proceedings. After all, it's hard to argue with someone when you're jumping and flailing your hands in the air. Try out a few different coping methods until you find one that effectively reduces anger.

When we reframe these tantrums as teachable moments, it becomes easier to deal with them and to talk our kids out of them. We can set aside our own frustration and instead focus on helping our kids rather than getting mad at them for things they can't quite control yet. The longer we practice these anger management strategies during tantrums, the fewer tantrums they will have.

STRATEGIES FOR MANAGING YOUR ANGER

Dealing with tantrums isn't the only time our anger might threaten to get the best of us. There are plenty of parenting experiences that can induce anger, frustration, and even rage if we're not careful about how we express our feelings. As a reminder, it's okay and natural to feel this way from time to time. If we have an aggravating or annoying experience, it's not surprising that we might feel angry. On top of that, it's not healthy to pretend we aren't feeling anger and shove it down inside us.

Still, just as we teach our kids when we correct their tantrums, there are acceptable and unacceptable ways to express that anger and unacceptable ways, especially in regards to how we expose our kids to our own anger. Remaining calm in difficult situations and redirecting anger in non-destructive ways are critical lessons if you are looking for a calmer parenting style.

By adopting strategies for anger management, you improve communication between you and your child.. You can demonstrate all the skills they need to center themselves in moments of agitation. In managing your own anger, you also manage your child's anger without any additional effort.

Change up Your Morning Routine

We tend to be in better moods when we start our days off right. They don't call being in a bad mood "waking up on the wrong side of the bed" for nothing!

The way we begin our day has a huge impact on how we feel the rest of the day. If we roll out of bed late, begin the day by fighting with our kids about getting ready, and automatically assume we're going to have bad experiences, we will definitely allow our self-fulfilling prophecy to come true. We'll end up stuck in a cycle of negativity that contributes to stress and more bouts of anger.

In order to eliminate this early-morning stress, we must shake up our mornings and start them out on the right foot. If you find yourself rushing around trying to get everything ready before everyone goes off to school or work, try shifting your sleep schedule so you go to bed half an hour earlier and wake up half an hour earlier. With the extra time, you can more comfortably manage all of your morning responsibilities. You'll also likely feel better rested by going to sleep a little earlier, meaning you'll have enough energy to calmly deal with a fussy child in the morning.

If you want to add a little more zen to your morning routine, plan a small, relaxing but fun activity for right after you wake up. Instead of rolling out of bed and scrambling to get ready, try taking just fifteen minutes to read a book or do a brief stretching exercise. You might even dedicate your morning to getting a workout in before everyone else is up and ready to distract you from your yoga or a quick jog around the block. Do something that centers your mind and energizes you, making you excited to wake up rather than dreading it. This makes it easier to go to bed in the evenings, as you know you always have something good to look forward to each day. If you start your morning out on this positive note, it sets the tone for the rest of the day.

It can be hard to find time for a real breakfast in the mornings. We may find ourselves rushing around and grabbing something unhealthy while hardly saying a word to our family. This can negatively impact our mood and overall health. If you can wake up a little early, use this extra time to make yourself and your family a real breakfast so you can eat together and bond at the breakfast table. Alternatively, adults could practice intermittent fasting, which typically involves skipping breakfast and only eating during certain windows each day. This has also been linked to some notable health benefits like weight loss and higher energy levels throughout the day. Either method is better than grabbing an unhealthy breakfast and rushing out the door, so try them both and see which works best for you and your family. The key is not to follow any particular diet but to try things out and find a healthful, positive routine everyone can stick with and enjoy over time.

Try Out Routine Meditation

We've already discussed the benefits of doing breathing exercises while we're in the heat of the moment, but it's also a good idea to turn meditation into part of your daily routine. It's a great addition to your early morning habits, but it can also be helpful to calm your mind shortly before bed, helping you shed the stresses of the day. Meditation has significant long-term benefits for our mentalities and outlooks on life. It teaches us to be more in tune with our breathing and our emotional state, which helps us be more mindful of our thoughts and feelings. Studies have shown that people who meditate consistently are more successful at "reducing stress, improving sleep, increasing focus, [and] improving relationships" (Headspace, n.d., para. 1). These are all great benefits if you're trying to live a more peaceful life and reduce the presence of volatile emotions that could harm your ability to communicate with your child.

You can practice a very simple meditation just by finding a calm, quiet place, closing your eyes, and focusing on your breath. After a few minutes of deep breathing, you'll feel more focused and centered. After a few days, you'll have a better grasp on your emotions, as well as how you can recognize them and change how you express them. If you're not especially great at holding yourself to meditation and you need some additional help, look for guided meditations online. You can find everything from general meditation routines to more specific routines on topics like gratitude, dealing with anger, or manifesting success. Whatever type of meditation you choose to practice, you'll get all the upsides that meditation can bring as long as you stick to it for just a few minutes each day.

Address Your Wants and Needs

As parents, we often get so wrapped up in our kids' wants and needs that we forget our own. We see them as less important than making sure our kids are attended to. However, unfulfilled wants and needs can interfere with our ability to be effective parents. If stress and anxiety are weighing us down, we'll be distracted and more prone to snapping in stressful situations. Our exhaustion and aggravation piles up. We need time to ourselves to decompress and unwind just like everyone else. This means taking time to do fun, enriching activities that alleviate stress on top of our other parenting duties.

Of course, while a spa day or a vacation might sound nice, parenting is a job that doesn't come with sick days or vacation hours. It can be hard to find the time to address our needs. If you're having difficulty staying refreshed and rejuvenated, there are a few solutions you can try to work around your kid's schedule. The first is to schedule "me time" for when your child is otherwise occupied. This might mean in the evenings after they go to bed, or during the day while they're at school, if you're not working during these hours. Even if you are, enjoying a nice lunch or chatting with coworkers can help you replenish some of your energy. If you have a spouse, partner, or someone else who is sharing parenting duties with you, make sure they're pulling their weight. If you're being saddled with the brunt of the parenting responsibility, you're going to get exhausted after a while, and you might even feel resentful of your partner. If you need to, have an honest conversation about how much effort they're making to raise your child and what you'd like to see them do to be more present in your child's life. When your spouse picks up some of the slack, this can leave you with more free time to decompress.

Your spouse isn't the only person who can watch your child for a while if you need to take a break. Ask other members of the family if they'd be willing to watch the kids for a while. You could also look into daycare services or enlist the help of a neighborhood babysitter. Even if you only for a few hours, you are giving yourself the opportunity to recharge your parenting batteries. Don't feel bad about needing some time to yourself. It doesn't make you a bad parent to still want to see a movie or read a book without having to rush away to put out a fire. So long as you remain present in your child's life, there's nothing wrong with taking a break every once in a while.

Finally, you can also seek out activities that you can do together with your child to let off a little steam. While kids can be a source of significant stress, more often than not they are still the light of our lives. Spending time with them can bring us joy just as much as spending time with our friends or other family members. If you need some time to destress, take your child to the movies, or go out to eat with them. Play a game together, solve a puzzle, or read to them. The list of activities that are fun for both parents and kids is endless, and engaging in these kinds of activities can strengthen your parent-child bond.

SET REALISTIC EXPECTATIONS

A common pitfall when trying to manage our anger comes in the form of setting our expectations too high for our kids. This means we expect too much of them for the amount of cognitive development they have experienced so far. We might expect our kids to remember rules we have laid down or routines we've established for them, but truly acquiring the skill or knowledge can take more practice than we might think. They may not fully understand what we're asking, or they might have trouble keeping their emotions in check if they're not old enough to master those skills yet. It's important for us to be patient with both our kids and ourselves. Some lessons will only take a few hours or days to learn, while others might take weeks or months of practice. If we go in with this mindset, we'll have a lot more patience when certain lessons take time for kids to internalize.

We might also put a lot of pressure on our kids to do well in school or an extracurricular activity. If our kids aren't great

at math right away, or if they're not the star of their li\.
league team, we might feel disappointed. We may even question our parenting skills, again falling into the trap of feeling
insecure about ourselves and lashing out in anger as a result.
We might get mad at our kids because we expect better
grades or better performance, even though we know they're
trying their best.

This can blind us to possible alternative solutions to these
problems, like tutoring, extra practice at home, and different
methods of teaching. When we learn to manage expectations and accept our kids for who they are, we can help them
improve without putting the burden of shame and failure on
their shoulders, or on our own. Try to set realistic expectations for your kid's behaviors and achievements and make
adjustments only if kids aren't quite hitting these reasonable
goals.

Improving our communication skills and our relationships
with our kids starts with improving ourselves. When we
manage our expectations, adjust our emotions, and moderate
our own tempers, we set a good example for our kids and
help them do the same. With these skills, we are ready to
help our kids master their emotions and have clear and positive conversations with us.

3

THE MISSING STEP IN MOST PARENTING RELATIONSHIPS

There are plenty of issues that can damage the relationship between parent and child. These issues might come in the form of a lack of trust, such as if your child lies to you about whether they broke something or the dog did it, or if your child doesn't feel they can trust you. Another common issue is a lack of understanding for each other. If you're not listening to what the other person has to say, you're not making an effort to meet them halfway as you would in other life conflicts. You may also have trouble laying down rules and getting kids to follow them, or getting your child to respect your authority as a parent without using methods that make them afraid of you. Each of these issues has the potential to damage or complicate the relationship between you and your child, which has the potential to harm their development.

If these issues aren't corrected early in a child's development, they can persist long into their teen and young-adult years, if not for the rest of their lives. Our early years have a huge part in determining who we're going to be as adults. If the way you interact with your younger child causes mistrust, you may end up with a teenager who is more likely to act out in destructive ways. They may embrace risky behaviors, and they misbehave even further if you react by tightening the reins without speaking to them about the issue. If you don't try to understand your child when they're young and you don't encourage them to open up to you, you may find your relationship fractured and distant later on. If you rely on strict punishments for bad behaviors rather than trying to talk about the issue and uncover the root of the problem, you may irreparably damage this relationship as your child grows to fear or even resent you. This is a frightening thing to think about for any parent, but if we allow ourselves to act out of uncontrolled anger and frustration, it could very well become a reality.

How do we fix these issues? How do we make sure we're giving our kids the best care we can, adequately preparing them for the rest of their lives? The key lies in looking at the common factor in all of the above issues: poor communication. A lack of communication is at the heart of these problems, and it will continue to bog down our personal relationships until we purposefully change the way we approach having a conversation with our kids. If we try to dominate the conversation, imposing our will and even threatening kids until they listen to us, we risk driving our kids away. If we never set any rules or boundaries, kids don't know what we expect from them, and they're more likely to keep pushing these invisible boundaries until they find the line they shouldn't cross. If we set boundaries but fail to appropriately convey these boundaries to our kids, any punishment we give them feels arbitrary and unearned in their eyes, because they don't know the rules. We haven't told them what those rules are. Whether we fail to set any rules, we fail to tell kids these rules or are too strict with our rules and don't let our kids be part of the conversation, we falter when it comes to communication. This sabotages our best efforts, all because we didn't understand how to talk to our kids.

While poor communication can be a serious problem in parent-child relationships, the good news is that it doesn't have to be this way. You can establish honest and clear communication with your child by changing your interactions with them. This single change will have a positive ripple effect that will eventually reach all areas of your child's life as they get older. Through first understanding the role of communication in your relationship with your child and then adopting strategies and habits that allow for good communication, you can strengthen your relationship and encourage your child's healthy development.

COMMUNICATION AND PARENTAL RELATIONSHIPS

If we've never spoken to someone before, we consider them a stranger. When we've talked to them a few times, they become an acquaintance. If there is compatibility, deeper and more personal conversations may lead to friendship. Developing relationships with our kids follows a similar pattern. If we don't communicate with kids, we remain "strangers," even if we live under the same roof. We don't get to really know our kids as individuals and deepen our bonds with them. It is only when we communicate with our kids that we begin to solidify the relationship.

Talking to our kids aids their development at every stage. Think back to when your child was a baby. They didn't understand what you were saying, but you probably still talked to them as if they could. Even though they might not know the meaning of the words, babies still pick up on our tone. They might ball up their fists and cry if they hear raised voices or a terse tone of voice, or they might giggle and smile along if our words are pleasant and playful. During these early months, our kids learn to communicate with us too.

They learn to tell us they're upset or scared by calling for us. They tell us they're curious and playful by moving their arms and legs. When a baby says their first word, it's typically treated as a momentous occasion, as it should be. This is proof that your child's communication skills are developing.

Now that our kids are older, we might not treat every new development milestone with the same gravitas. We probably don't make a scrapbook entry when our kids first talk to us about their feelings or resolve their first argument with a friend. But these moments are no less important, as communication is critical at every stage. Everything we teach our kids through the way we communicate with them is a lesson they internalize and emulate. If we pay attention to our kids' communication skills and the way we talk to them, we can see the direct impact of our words and actions on their development.

How Poor Communication Can Negatively Impact Development

Unfortunately, not all methods of communication are positive and healthy. If we struggle to communicate effectively with our kids, they could have trouble in various areas of their development.

We use language as a way to get to know each other. If we don't talk to each other, we may not ever fully understand who our kids are, and our kids can feel equally distant from us. They may be uncertain about being open and vulnerable with us because they haven't learned these skills. We don't form the same close connection that we could if only we knew how to listen and speak effectively. This may create a painful rift between parent and child that can, in some cases, keep kids from forming a genuine emotional bond with us.

We're not the only ones affected by communication issues. If we don't pass along the skills our kids need to form and maintain relationships with us, they can have difficulty forming and maintaining relationships with their peers. They may be unable to deal effectively with conflicts, and may resort to yelling or hitting to get their way. They may also have trouble speaking honestly to their friends, which can become an issue as kids get older and talk about more serious problems in their lives. If kids lack the skills necessary to connect to other kids their age, they may find themselves struggling to make friends and further develop their social skills. Additionally, they may have more trouble at school because they struggle with the communication skills necessary for education. They may not adequately develop the listening skills needed to pay attention in class, or they may have trouble communicating their thoughts and answering questions on homework and quizzes. Academic difficulties at an early age could continue well into their academic career if they never build up their communication skills.

Another area that is often negatively impacted by poor communication skills is self-esteem. Good communication and close bonds with friends can help ward off low self-esteem issues in kids. When kids struggle to make friends, or if they perform poorly in school as a result of their inability to listen, their self-confidence can suffer. Kids who have unaddressed communication needs "often see themselves as less able and less popular than their friends" (The Communication Trust, n.d., para. 7). Poor self-esteem in kids could keep them from reaching their full potential and living a happy life. It can contribute to mental health issues later in life and interfere with your child's ability to form healthy relationships in the future.

While each of these potential negative impacts can be scary to think about, it's important to know about them so you can take the steps necessary to avoid them. By building up your kids' communication skills, you ensure they're able to form a healthy parent-child relationship, as well as relationships with their friends and educators. This encourages their development and keeps them from falling behind other kids their age.

ADVANTAGES OF GOOD COMMUNICATION

If you can avoid the pitfalls of lackluster communication and instead practice good communication skills as a parent, the benefits are tremendous. For one, you get to avoid each of the unfortunate side effects of poor communication. This means kids are better at forming relationships and are more likely to do well in school. Kids who are taught good communication skills are also more likely to have a positive relationship with their parents. This positive relationship develops because kids understand what it means to be respectful in a relationship where both parties feel seen and heard. They also become more comfortable with their role in the family and the rules they're expected to follow. They understand more about themselves and their feelings, and they know when it's appropriate to act a certain way and when it's not.

As your child learns each of these lessons, they will start to see you not just as their parent but also as someone they can trust and rely on. They will look to you for advice, and they will be more likely to listen to you as long as you maintain this standard of effective communication. The simple arts of talking and listening pave the way for healthy development and healthy relationships for kids.

. . .

Building Mutual Respect

When most people think of respect in the parent-child dynamic, they generally think of kids being respectful toward their parents. To be sure, this is an important aspect of your relationship to establish. If your child doesn't respect you, they're not going to listen when you tell them to do things. They might question your authority, talk back, and go against your wishes because they feel like they "can." When your child respects you, they're more likely to listen even when they don't fully understand why you're asking them to clean up their toys or go to bed on time. However, the respect in your relationship shouldn't be one-sided. If you want your child to respect you, you also have to show them respect.

Just like in many other aspects of parenting, it is up to us to model the behaviors we want to see in our kids. If we want to show them how to be respectful, we must be respectful toward them too.

Many parents make the mistake of demanding respect from their kids without showing them the same courtesy. They see themselves as "the boss" and they want to be listened to without discussion or objection, but this just isn't how a healthy relationship works. While you will need to put your foot down as a parent, you can do this while still being respectful of your kid's needs, their boundaries, and their feelings. In fact, by showing your child respect, they will mimic your behavior. They'll be more receptive to your guidance and more willing to listen, all because you showed them they're worthy of your respect, and you're worthy of theirs.

One way to show your child the basics of respect is to give them autonomy. When kids are young, we want to do everything for them. We tend to resist the idea of letting our kids take care of themselves or make their own decisions. After all, we're the parents; we're responsible for their safety. This is fine when they're not old enough to make these choices themselves, but eventually our kids will start establishing boundaries for personal comfort and privacy. If we try to intrude upon these boundaries, often by being "helicopter parents" who insist kids wear a certain outfit, for example, or or talk over them in conversations. It's hard to relinquish this control, but we have to accept that our kids are learning and growing every day. If we don't give them the space to start making small decisions about their likes, dislikes, and what they're comfortable with, they're going to start feeling like we don't care about their feelings.

Encourage your child to start out by making small decisions for themselves. When they're old enough to get themselves dressed, let them choose between a few different outfits rather than just deciding on one yourself. Eventually, they'll be able to pick out clothes that help them express their unique personality and style, helping them affirm their sense of self. If possible, let your child have a space that is entirely their own, where they can go to cool down if they need to. This can help them feel more secure when they're still learning to control their emotions.

If they get themselves in trouble at school because of bad behavior, resist the urge to call up the teacher and bail them out. You can show them you sympathize, but it's important for them to take responsibility for their mistakes. Show them you value their opinions. They'll become more independent, not to mention more likely to treat you with respect. You'll form a bond based not on fear of your authority but on mutual respect and love, which is a far stronger force.

Helping Kids Understand Themselves

Growing up can be confusing for kids. They're constantly experiencing and learning about the world around them, and this information can be hard to process. Perhaps nothing is quite as difficult for kids to understand as themselves. Since kids' brains are still developing at this stage, their sense of self is continually developing too. They likely don't fully understand their own feelings and how to handle them, let alone who they are as a person. You can assist them in this process by helping them recognize and explain their feelings. When they're able to identify these feelings, they can take steps to react appropriately.

You can encourage greater emotional maturity for your child just by talking to them. If you notice your child getting upset, sit down with them and ask them to identify how they're feeling. If they're struggling, you can ask them, "Do you feel sad because of what happened? Did it make you angry?" You can provide the words they need to describe their feelings, but let them decide how they feel on their own. Once they do, help them understand what part of the situation made them feel that way. Maybe they got frustrated because they were trying to read something but couldn't sound out the words. If they got upset while playing, something about their game might have startled them.

Identifying the root of the problem in words is important for kids, even if the cause of their anger or sadness is obvious to you. They might not have made the connection, and they need frequent practice so they can start thinking about what made them feel a certain way. Then they can decide how they want to handle the emotion. Help them build their problem-solving skills by asking them what they think they should do to calm down, providing suggestions when necessary.

Finally, help them find a solution to the problem when you can. If they were getting frustrated trying to read, help them sound out the words that were giving them trouble. If they were bothered by something in their game, play with them for a bit or remove the thing that scared them. Remember: just because it seems trivial to you doesn't mean it is for your child. Try to think about being agitated yourself—then imagine a far more powerful person laughing at you or otherwise invalidating your feelings. This step shows your child that getting upset doesn't have to mean the situation is unsolvable. They can step away from the situation, calm down, ask for help, and return to the task

When you encourage your child to talk about their feelings, you also build up their self-esteem. If kids never feel in control of themselves, they can struggle with their self-esteem. They may also have a hard time interacting with other kids their age, which can contribute to feelings of loneliness and low self-worth. If they learn to understand their feelings, they will begin constructing a more stable sense of self. They will be able to decide how they react to their feelings and their social skills will improve. Each of these benefits helps them improve their self-esteem and feel more comfortable and in control of themselves.

Solidifying Your Relationship

Finally, improving communication between you and your child will improve your relationship. If you can't talk to each other and discuss your honest feelings about a situation, your relationship can suffer. If your child feels like they should hide things from you for fear of punishment, or if they strain the relationship by having constant tantrums and yelling to get their way, it's tough to have a bond deeper than a relatively surface-level connection. You might start to feel almost alienated from your child's life, and they might think of you as a distant parental figure rather than a warm and loving one.

When you have good communication, the barriers between the two of you fall away. You grow closer to each other and you genuinely enjoy spending time with your child and learning about the person they're becoming.

With good communication, you're able to listen to your kid's needs. This helps you more adequately address them. If your child is struggling in a certain area, like school or relationships, listen to what they say when they talk about these aspects of their life, then see if you can guide them toward an answer. If your child is argumentative, listen to why they disagree with you. Even if you remain firm in asking your child to do something they disagree with, as you must sometimes as a parent, you still show them that you consider their input when making a decision.

As a parent, you must clearly communicate your expectations. If kids don't know what's off-limits and what's okay, they won't be able to practice good behavior because they won't know what good behavior looks like. Remain consistent with your rules and make sure your child knows exactly what rules they should be following. This lets them better understand the expectations you've set and their expectations as a member of the family. They will become more cooperative, and when they behave badly they'll understand why that behavior was wrong and, by extension, that a reasonable, constructive correction may be justified. All of this leads to an improved relationship that is free of the stresses that plague other parental relationships. The only difference is communication.

SIMPLE TECHNIQUES FOR IMPROVING COMMUNICATION

We know now why communication matters, so let's put that knowledge into practice. We communicate with our kids dozens if not hundreds of times throughout the day, often nonverbally. This means we have plenty of opportunities to readdress our communication strategies and improve them. These changes don't have to be huge. They can be minor changes we make in the way we speak and listen each day.

We will go into more detail about methods for improving communication in later chapters. For now, we will just look at a few simple tricks and techniques you can use to improve communication with your child. Keep in mind that while each of these strategies can be helpful, they may not all be helpful for every child. You know your child best, so choose strategies you think they will respond to. Feel free to try out a few different strategies to determine which ones work best.

Show Interest

First and perhaps most importantly, you cannot be a passive listener. If your child is excited to tell you what happened at school today and you respond with half-hearted "uh-huhs" while they're talking, they're going to pick up on how disinterested you sound. If you continue to do another activity while they're talking like watching TV or working, you're not giving your child your full attention. This means you aren't really listening, which is a barrier to communication. Kids will pick up on this even if you try to be sneaky about checking your phone in the middle of their ramble. When your mind is elsewhere, your child learns that whatever they have to say isn't worth listening to. This can make them more reluctant to open up to you in the future.

It can often be hard to make time for our kids in the busy world we live in. Kids tend to barge in with little regard for whatever we are doing at the time. You might be overworked and stressed, but remember that your child doesn't fully understand this yet. All they see when you ignore their story in favor of your work is that they are less important to you, and this isn't the message you want to convey. Instead, either ask them to wait a moment while you finish up, or set your task down so you can give your child your attention. Don't pick it up again until the conversation is over. When appropriate, ask encouraging questions as they speak, less to learn more about the situation and more to let them know you're engaged in the story. This teaches kids that you care about what they have to say. It also helps you understand your child better, as you pay more attention to what they want to tell you about their day or their feelings.

Avoid Knee-Jerk Reactions

Poor communication is most common when we don't give ourselves time to process new information. We might react to bad news automatically, which can lead to us leaping right to anger and shouting before we've had a chance to cool off and think about the situation logically. This can leave us regretting our words and actions an hour later, when our emotions have calmed down and we realize we didn't react how we should have.

Let's consider an example to showcase how important it is to evaluate the situation before responding. Let's say your child comes home from school on the day they got their math test back. They hand it to you, and you see that they didn't do very well at all. You might be tempted to get angry at them for not paying attention in class or not trying their best. You might punish them by sending them to their room or revoking toy privileges until they improve their grades.

But what does this really teach your child? They learn to fear the idea of telling you about the struggles they're having in school. They learn that poor performance makes you angry and can lead to punishment. Next time they get a bad grade, they might try to hide it or lie about it. Punishing them for a bad grade doesn't actually help them improve their math skills, especially if your punishments target privileges that aren't contributing to the bad grade. These are all outcomes that you might have anticipated if you'd had a minute to think about the situation. If you react immediately upon seeing the test score, you're more likely to just yell and punish without thinking of the long-term consequences.

Now let's revisit the scenario. Let's say that instead of instantly getting angry and losing your temper, you take a moment to calm down before addressing the test score. You take a few deep breaths, and you remind yourself that there's no reason to get defensive over your parenting skills because of one bad test grade. Now, you might ask your child, "What parts of this test were hard for you? Can I help explain them to you? Why do you think you didn't do well?" If your child shows genuine interest in improving their grades with your support, praise their efforts, not just the results of those efforts. This time around, you're actually addressing the underlying causes of why the bad grade occurred, and you're creating a strategy for improving your child's focus. This will help them more in the long run than yelling ever would.

Encourage Your Child and Reinforce a Positive Self-Image

Regardless of how our kids behave, we still love them. We love the amazing people they are and the people we watch them become as they grow up and learn new things. The parent-child bond is incredibly strong, and it can withstand even the loudest temper tantrums. That being said, while our kids likely feel the same love toward us that we feel toward them, they might have trouble trusting us if we don't communicate this to them. Don't be afraid to tell your child things that might seem obvious from your perspective, such as that you love them and that you're proud of them. Kids need to hear these affirmations from time to time to really internalize them. They need to know that you're on their side no matter what. This can help fill in the gaps created by poor or unreliable communication. In that case, if you lose your temper and yell, your child will still know you love them and didn't mean to get so upset. You will be able to move on from the incident because you have made your child feel secure in your relationship with them.

It's also important to encourage and appreciate your child's efforts. If you can see they're putting a lot of effort into not losing their temper, thank them for being so patient and understanding, even if they slip up a little. Let them know when they do a good job, reinforcing this behavior—

acknowledging good behavior can be just as useful as criticizing bad behavior. Praise their efforts regardless of results. This teaches kids that making an effort is worth doing in and of itself. It also teaches them not to stress too much about perfection.

We are imperfect, flawed creatures, and it's okay for kids to mess up sometimes, just as we might mess up sometimes as parents. It doesn't make us bad people, and it doesn't make us unworthy of love. Mistakes are just a part of life, and it's okay for us and our kids to make them. Encourage your child to put in the effort to improve and show them you're happy to see their communication skills develop.

Involve Kids in Decision-Making When Appropriate

Finally, let kids know they have a voice and a say in what happens just like everyone else in the family. We sometimes have the desire to just tell kids what's happening and how we're going to do things without seeking or seriously considering their point of view. Rather than letting them express some agency, we tell them exactly how things are going to go and what they're going to do. When this doesn't align with what our kids want to do, they resist and create avoidable conflict. When you can, try to involve kids in the decision-making process, or at the very least explain to them why they have to do a certain action. Let them make small but not-insignificant choices and talk to them about why they're expected to act a certain way. When you do, kids will become better listeners, and they'll get experience making their own choices. This often makes them more responsible as they get older because they are used to making decisions and exercising their problem-solving skills.

Of course, not every decision can be left up to kids. If you let your child decide what you ate for every meal, you might end up having pizza and candy for dinner for an entire week. However, there are still many circumstances where it's important for kids to exercise their voice.

For instance, you can ask them how they like dinner and find out more about their food preferences. If they really like meatloaf but aren't a big fan of turkey, try to accommodate their preferences the same way you would accommodate your own.

Keep meals healthy, but try not to force kids to eat something they just don't like; instead, look for other options and encourage them to try new foods. You could ask what kind of vegetable they want with their meal. If kids choose a vegetable they like, they're more likely to eat it, which can help a lot with picky eaters. It also lets your child feel like they have some control over what they put into their body, and that you respect their opinions. This is the foundation of good communication with not just your child but anyone in your life.

4

SO HOW DO YOU GET YOUR CHILD
TO LISTEN TO YOU ?

Previously, we discussed strategies that involved learning how to listen to your child and adapt to their needs. We have covered how to resist anger and speak to our kids in a way they'll understand. We have focused on ourselves. Now, we're going to shift our focus to our kids and try to see things from their point of view.

We're going to take steps and implement strategies that encourage our kids to treat us with the same respect we're trying to show them. After all, it takes two active participants to have a conversation. If we're talking but our kids aren't listening, we're going to have the same communication issues we would have if our kids are talking and we weren't listening.

In this chapter, we'll cover a few different reasons why our kids might not be listening to us. We're also going to take a look at what we can do to resolve these issues when we encounter them, and how we can encourage our kids to be better listeners. It's important to note that the roadblocks to listening listed in this chapter do not account for any potential medical conditions or developmental disorders that might be impacting your child's ability to respond to directions. These issues can affect a child's hearing or their comprehension. If you believe your child may have one of these conditions, discuss the situation with a medical professional or child development specialist and follow their advice.

WHY KIDS MAY REFUSE TO LISTEN

Kids might not listen to us for a variety of different reasons. We tend to ascribe the behavior to plain old stubbornness or purposeful bad behavior. While kids are certainly capable of both , more often than not there is a reason behind their behavior. There is usually something keeping them from giving us their full attention, or there may be a previous incident that continues to influence how our kids are acting. These underlying causes can be hard to spot, especially if we are quick to jump to labeling it as simple defiance and even quicker to punish our kids for not listening. Taking a moment to try to identify the reasoning behind kids' stubborn or disrespectful behavior can help us deescalate a situation before it can turn into an argument. It also teaches us what conditions to look out for next time our kids are behaving badly so we can reduce the likelihood of the problem repeating itself.

Some of the reasons for a child's lack of listening skills have to do with how we talk to them and what we're saying. Other reasons might include what is currently going on around them, their own desires, and how we have acted in the past. Consider each of these areas as potential sources of stubborn behavior and try to identify which might be negatively influencing your child.

We Are Saying Too Much at Once

Kids aren't able to multitask or mentally juggle many things at once. If we give them too much to remember, they may struggle to keep up with it. For example, if you tell your child five or more rules at once, they might let one slip from their mind if they're not thinking about it. They might remember one or two, but they'll probably forget the others unless you make an effort to consistently remind them. It's not that they don't want to listen to you or obey your rules. Rather, they get overwhelmed and simply forget.

Imagine you're trying to tell your child to do a few chores around the house. Let's say that in one scenario, you give them the list of things to do all at the same time. You ask them to clean their room, pick up their toys in the living room, and get their laundry together to be washed. In the other scenario, you let them know you're going to ask them to do a few chores, but you assign the tasks one at a time and don't tell them to do the next task until they've finished the previous one. Which scenario do you think is going to turn out better? In the first one, your child might start cleaning up their room, but they'll probably get distracted before they can pick up their toys, let alone get their laundry together. In much the same way that you might forget to pick something up at the store if you don't have a way to reference your list, your child might forget the next task without meaning to. In the second scenario, there is no opportunity for your child to forget what's expected of them because you're not over-loading them with directions. You're spelling things out for them in a clear and easy-to-follow way, and they're following through.

If you want your child to follow the rules, clarity and simplicity are key. Remind kids of the rules when you know they'll be relevant. For example, if you have a rule about no muddy shoes in the house, it's a good idea to restate this rule when it's raining and your child wants to go out and play. Repetition is a great way to make a complex list more easily memorized for kids. You can also try alternate memorization methods, like making a list and hanging it up on the wall or turning the rules into a song that will stick in kids' heads.

Just try not to overload them or give conflicting instructions, and you will find that kids have a much easier time remembering what's expected of them.

They Are Distracted

Kids have fairly short attention spans. They usually find it difficult to concentrate on tasks that don't interest them, and they may have trouble paying attention to directions if there are a lot of other things going on at the same time. You've probably seen for yourself just how short your kid's attention span can be. You've just gotten them settled with some crayons and paper, you leave the room for half a second, and when you come back they're onto some new activity. This brief attention span can cause difficulty following rules and listening, as there may be some other activity that looks more interesting to them.

Distractibility is only amplified by modern technology and toys. If you're trying to talk to your child but they're watching a TV show, playing a video game, or messing with a toy while you're speaking, they're not giving you their full attention. This means they're more likely to ignore what you're saying in favor of the fun toy or game.

There are a few solutions you can try for this. One is to make sure you have their kid's attention by asking them to pause their game and listen. Only ask them to do something when you know they're actually paying attention to what you're saying. Another method is to make the activity you want them to do fun so they naturally want to listen. If you turn clean-up time into a game or contest, your child is more likely to give it their attention instead of getting distracted by more fun tasks.

We Are Distracted

We can be just as distracted as our kids sometimes. As parents, we have to juggle a lot of tasks and responsibilities at the same time. In the morning alone, we might have to worry about breakfast and packing lunches, getting the kids up and ready for school, and getting ourselves ready for our days all at the same time, and our to-do list may only get more crowded from there. With so many thoughts running through our heads and so many tasks we need to do each day, it's hard not to be distracted when we're talking to our kids. But distraction gets in the way of good communication. It keeps us from paying attention to what we're saying and how we're saying it, which can lead to miscommunication and sometimes hurt feelings if we say or do something without thinking about the consequences.

To get the best response from your child, make sure you are giving them the same attention they are giving you. Try not to yell instructions across the house. If you can, pause what you're doing and make sure your child is looking at you before asking them to do anything.

We Are Using Harsh Language

The language we use when we're talking is often more important than what we're trying to say. If we're trying to tell someone they're doing a task incorrectly, they're more likely to listen to us if we gently correct them rather than criticizing the way they're currently doing the task. We tend to soften our tone when we're talking to other adults, but we can sometimes forget this when we're talking to our kids. Of course, it's equally important to pay attention to the language we use in both situations.

Kids may be more resistant to what we're telling them if our words feel like criticism or if we make them feel foolish for doing it wrong. If our first impulse is to laugh or mock, we should pause and consider our words more carefully. If your child is doing something incorrectly, instead of saying "you're wrong," try saying "this way is better." Your child is less likely to get defensive and upset, and more likely to try out the new, better method.

We Are Too Passive or Too Assertive

The most effective form of communication is the middle ground between passive and assertive. If we command our kids to do something, they might resist just because they feel we're being unfair. Making many demands or promising strict punishment if our kids don't comply can make them resent us over time. On the other hand, pleading with our kids to follow the rules undermines our authority. Either option will result in kids who learn not to listen to directions.

Strike a balance between these two extremes. Remain firm when you ask your child to do something, but avoid outright ordering them to do it. Don't cave to your child's desire or lack of desire to follow your rules, but don't immediately escalate the situation to something more aggressive when it doesn't need to be so confrontational. As an example, let's say you want your child to finish their homework. If you say "Finish your work or else!" they'll feel bullied into listening, but if you say "Could you please, please work on your home-work?" your child might feel like they don't need to follow your instructions. Instead, try something like, "It's time to work on your homework." This provides direction without leaving room for unreasonable arguments, and at the same time doesn't feel quite as commanding. You can also try explaining why getting their homework done is important so they'll feel more compelled to complete it on their own in the future.

We Don't Follow Through

If our kids ignore us, we need to show them we are serious about our rules. This means following our words with actions. If you ask your child to follow an instruction and they continue to refuse, follow through with an appropriate punishment. If they won't pick up their toys, let them know they won't be getting one of their toys back until they clean up. If they aren't listening to you, a time out may be an appropriate punishment.

One important thing to keep in mind when deciding on consequences for your child's actions is to avoid lashing out in anger. You might be so worked up about your child's behavior that your immediate reaction is to yell, hit, or exaggerate the punishment in comparison to the offense. However, these are not appropriate punishments, and they don't help your child learn to behave. Punishments given out of anger are typically too harsh and often scare kids rather than teach them. If you feel yourself getting upset, take a moment to calm down before you decide on a consequence.

EXERCISES FOR ENCOURAGING KIDS TO LISTEN

Invite your child to take an active role in developing their own listening skills. Changing the way you interact with your child is only half of the solution to bad behavior. The other half is getting your child to practice their listening skills and their own ability to communicate. You can accomplish this by engaging them in exercises that encourage their participation and development. Try out some of these approaches with your child and take notice of how they help you improve your communication with each other.

Speak Face-to-Face

Our faces are incredibly expressive. If someone speaks to us with their face turned away, it's harder to know how they feel. We can listen to the tone of their voice, but we miss out on a lot if we can't make that face-to-face connection.

When we talk to our kids, we should try to make the same connection. This means looking at each other while talking and getting down to their level. We want to eliminate any barriers that could be making communication more difficult, and this is a great way to do it. When we look our kids in the eyes and encourage them to do the same, we make sure everyone is giving the conversation their full attention. We also teach our kids to respectfully listen when someone's talking.

Listen to Your Child

If we want our kids to be good communicators, we have to show them how to listen. Practice giving your child your attention and taking an interest in what they have to say. When we showcase these good practices, our kids will subconsciously replicate them. They'll understand how to be good listeners when they see you setting a good example.

On top of being a good role model, listening can help you understand how kids process events. You'll learn more about who your child is and where they might be experiencing difficulties with their ability to communicate. For example, you might notice that certain topics seem to halt communication. Maybe your child is all too excited to tell you about what they did during recess, but they clam up when you ask about what they learned in class. This might suggest they're having trouble in one of their classes. Other times, you might pick up on your child's difficulties expressing certain emotions. They may have trouble putting their fear or anger into words, which you might not have noticed if you hadn't made the effort to listen more carefully. Once you know where the difficulties are, you can take steps to fix them, whether that means looking into tutoring options or helping them label their feelings.

Figure Out What's Causing Conflict

Disobedience is rarely the result of stubbornness alone. Kids who don't tend to listen to their parents often have stress in their lives that could be contributing to the issue, or there may be something holding them back from completing certain tasks. If you never ask your child why they don't want to do what you ask, you might miss out on a chance to directly address the underlying issue.

Speak to your child and try to figure out why they're not following instructions. Maybe there's something they don't understand about the task you've given them, or maybe they don't understand why the task is necessary. Clearing up these issues means that next time you want them to do the same task, you'll face less resistance.

Keep Your Cool

As we previously discussed, losing our cool can make it a lot harder to get our kids to listen to us. If they feel like they're being unfairly yelled at, they'll be less inclined to see why the task or rule is necessary. If you feel yourself getting angry when your child isn't listening, breathe deeply and stay calm. Avoid shouting at your child, as this can make them even more uncooperative. Use a calm but firm tone of voice when you speak to them, and treat them as you would want to be treated in return.

Explain Why They're Not Being Respectful

Kids may be disrespectful without realizing the harm it causes. When they choose to ignore you, they might not notice how it makes you feel. They also may not have a good grasp on what's considered polite and respectful behavior yet. Sit them down and explain to them that ignoring someone when they're talking is hurtful. Talk about how it's frustrating when they don't listen. Don't be afraid to show emotional vulnerability. Talking about your feelings can encourage them to open up about their own.

If your child is still having a tough time understanding why what they're doing is wrong, you can try turning the tables with a short exercise. Let your child know ahead of time that for about 10 minutes, you won't be listening to anything they say. Make sure your child understands that this is just an exercise to show them how you feel when they don't listen to you. By the time the 10 minutes are up, your child will understand that it hurts to be ignored. (Obviously, don't do anything that might seriously frighten or upset the child.) They will know how you feel when they choose to ignore you, and they will think twice about ignoring you in the future.

Make Listening Fun

Sometimes kids ignore us because there's something more fun they'd like to do instead. If you feel like you're constantly battling for your child's attention, try making the task you want them to do equally or more fun than what they're doing. If you want them to clean up their room, try timing it and letting them see how quickly they can put their toys away. If you'd like them to do their chores, make a chore chart and reward them when they've successfully completed their chores for a certain number of days in a row. This gives your child an incentive to listen to you and cooperate with you. When they see these tasks as fun, they'll often complete them without any complaints.

Don't Expect Overnight Results

Finally, give your child the time they need to adjust to new rules and develop listening skills. Your child isn't going to go from ignoring you to listening to every word you say overnight. Kids need enough time to get used to these new ideas and rules—especially when they are larger in scope—before they can put them into practice. Be patient with your child and work with them if they start to fall back into old habits. If you gradually introduce them to tasks and activities that will improve their listening skills, they're more likely to adopt permanent good listening habits. This will be more beneficial in the long run for their communication skills.

5

START DOING THIS AND WATCH WHAT HAPPENS IN 7 DAYS !

In this chapter, we'll take a look at some of the best methods for improving communication with your child. You'll learn about different exercises and activities you can use to encourage your child to better understand their emotions, understand how to handle strong emotions, and calm themselves when they're upset. You'll also learn about different tips to get your child to speak more frequently and more honestly about any difficulties they may be facing and might need help with. This chapter also includes methods for improving your own communication skills for talking with kids based on the information you have learned thus far about child development. These exercises will improve communication between you and your child, ultimately leading to fewer arguments and a deeper parent-child bond.

Each of these methods have been proven to improve communication with young kids. They are strategies and techniques that have consistently led to significant results and, in some cases, have been the catalyst for a more positive and genuine parent-child relationship. However, while each of these methods are worth trying, it's important to keep in mind that not every method will work for every child. Some kids may not respond as well to a strategy as others, and that's okay. Every child is unique, and it's alright if you go through a few different strategies before you find what works for you. Be patient, repeat the methods as necessary, and pay attention to how your child responds to each new strategy you try. If you notice an improvement in listening and communicating skills, you're on the right track. If they're still having difficulty paying attention and following your directions, try another one of these tips. While this trial-and-error process can be a little frustrating at times, it is necessary to ensure you are using the best strategies.

METHODS FOR IMPROVING COMMUNICATION

The way we approach teaching our kids better communication skills directly impacts how good at communication they will be. We are role models for our kids, and while they will learn a lot from their teachers, other guardians, and peers, most emotional education occurs inside the home. If we set a good example for our kids and we give them the tools they need to be good communicators, they will have an easier time excelling in other areas of their lives.

The following methods are specifically tailored to teach our kids everything they need to know to form and maintain healthy relationships. When they learn to listen carefully, weigh their responses, and articulate their feelings, they will have more success in conversations with adults and other kids alike. They will be able to understand and explain their emotions to others without confrontation, and accept our gentle correction of the way they choose to express their emotions, which leads to better solutions without tears. They will listen better not because they are afraid to ignore us, but because they want to make us happy and proud—and because we want to do the same for them.

Talk During Downtime

Previously, we have discussed the importance of making sure you have your child's full attention when you're asking them to do something. While this is important when we want to be sure they're listening to us, these aren't the only kinds of conversations we want to have with our kids. We also want to be open and honest with them, and able to speak comfortably about a wide variety of topics. We can speak to our kids no matter what we're doing, whether we're in the car, at the store, or just relaxing around the house.

If you have some downtime when neither you nor your child is doing much more than busywork, fill the gaps with conversation. Talk to them while you're making dinner or driving them home from school. Ask them about their day, and talk about anything fun or interesting that happened during yours. Invite them to give their opinions on different topics, including arbitrary things like how they enjoyed their lunch or what their favorite movie is and why. The simple act of encouraging more frequent conversation can greatly improve your relationship with your child as you start to learn more about who they are and what they enjoy. You should be able to talk to your child as comfortably as you would a good friend. Show a genuine interest in getting to know them and they'll want to talk to you too.

Create Talking Rituals

We all have times when we're receptive to conversation. If you wake up groggy in the morning and haven't had your coffee yet, you might only give short, terse answers to any questions you're asked. If you're exhausted after work, it's possible that the last thing you want to do is answer a flurry of questions, but it's also possible that you'd prefer the opportunity to vent about the tough parts of your day. You might also get annoyed if you feel like you're getting interrupted in the middle of your story with too many questions, or if someone doesn't show enough interest in what you're saying. Conversation style preferences can vary from person to person, and maintaining a good relationship typically involves adapting to the other person's style of talking.

Our kids also have conversational preferences. They may be more open to talking after school, or they might be especially chatty in the mornings. They might enjoy being asked about their day, or they might prefer to guide the topic of conversation themselves so they can talk about what they enjoy and avoid the things that made them frustrated. Picking up on their preferences can help you have more beneficial conversations with less arguing. In particular, get a feeling for when your child is most chatty and how involved they'd like you to be in the conversation. Some kids are content to ramble with less input from you, while others need coaxing to feel reassured that you care about what they have to say. If you keep interrupting a rambling child to ask about small details, you might frustrate them. If you don't respond to a child who needs a bit more prompting to speak, they might get discouraged and trail off. Either misstep can halt the conversation in its tracks and make kids more resistant to listening in the future.

Identifying and adapting to these preferences can help you avoid the hidden landmines that can derail conversations and lead to hurt feelings and frustration.

Be Genuine

Parents often want to make sure they're responding to their kids in the "right" way. To this end, we will often adjust our natural responses to sound more encouraging or less negative. For example, if our child says they weren't asked to play at lunch by their friend, we might immediately jump to saying "That's horrible! They should be ashamed. I'm calling the teacher right now," even if this interference and intrusion in our child's personal life is more detrimental than it is helpful. On the other hand, we might play down our response with a simple "Oh, that's sad," which can make our child feel like we're not listening to their concerns.

We want to know what the best reaction is to anything our children tells us, and we often worry that saying the wrong thing could hamper communication. While saying cruel or uncaring things would certainly get in the way of healthy communication, often the best advice is the same given in almost any social situation: be yourself. You only need to be honest and genuine in your responses.

Exaggerating or understating your responses can make conversations feel stilted and awkward. When you do this, you're not trying to connect; you're trying to analyze your child and come up with the best response. This is exhausting and unnecessary. Your child isn't your boss. While you do need to pay attention to what you say, you don't have to carefully curate your response out of fear of being fired or other consequences. Speak your mind when your child talks to you, as this tells them you're interested in what they're saying. This way, they'll want to share more.

Pay Attention to Details

When we tell a story, we want to know that the other person is listening. If we spend a long time talking about everything we did on our last vacation, it's frustrating to talk to the same person a few days later and have them ask if we saw a certain landmark. We know that while they were ostensibly giving us their attention, they weren't really paying close attention to what we were saying. Maybe they were distracted by something they were doing or had other things on their mind, but it can still make us feel hurt because we know they didn't really listen to us.

Our kids want to know we're listening to them too. If they start to tell a story, try to follow along as closely as you can. Kids' stories can sometimes be told in a complex, somewhat scattered way, but if we really pay attention we can usually get a better picture of what our kids are trying to tell us. Paying attention to the details can also help us uncover details that our kids didn't mention. For example, if we notice they said they were playing with someone as recess who they don't usually mention, we might ask why that is. They might say they made a new friend, or they might reveal that they're in an argument with their usual playmate. This is important information that we would have missed out on if we didn't listen to the details of their story and ask questions.

Use "Door Opener" Statements

"Door opener" statements are simple words and phrases that show your conversation partner that you're interested in what they're saying. These phrases are meant to "open the door" to continued conversation, inviting the other person to step inside and keep talking. They're easy ways to ask for more information, react to what you're being told, and respect the other person's time and opinions. Door opener statements include phrases like "That's interesting," "Really?" and even a simple "Uh-huh" or "M-hm" in between sentences. While these phrases don't really add much to the conversation from an informational standpoint, they can help facilitate conversation by showing your child you're paying attention. They also encourage you to keep your mind on the conversation, as you have to respond rather than just passively taking in information.

Door opener statements are an important part of active listening. When we listen passively to someone else, we don't contribute to the conversation. When we're active listeners, we may speak back and forth with someone else, or we might find another less verbal or non-verbal way to get involved.

To understand the idea better, imagine a classroom. If the teacher stands at the board and lectures for an hour, the kids are listening passively. They might start out interested, but after a while that interest might fade away as they get distracted or disinterested. They might start doodling in their notebooks or daydreaming about playing outside, since they're no longer part of the conversation. On the other hand, if the teacher invites their class to answer questions, ask questions of their own when they don't understand something, and take notes, this encourages active listening. Kids pay more attention when they feel like they're part of the conversation, and so do adults. Even waiting for the right time to add an "M-hm" keeps our brains focused on what the other person is saying. Active listening can also involve making eye contact and nodding or shaking our heads. When we listen actively, we're more likely to pay attention and retain the information.

Sprinkling some door opener statements into a conversation can help us keep our focus on the other person and ensure that when it's our turn to talk, we're ready to participate.

Use More 'Dos' Than 'Don'ts'

It's a lot easier to know what you don't want your child to do than what you want them to do. You know you don't want your child to argue with you, make a mess, or act disrespectfully toward other family members or teachers.

Because of this, it's easy to make rules about what behaviors we want them to avoid. However, it can be a little harder to identify what we'd like our kids to do instead. Telling our kids what not to do can make them feel restricted by rules without giving them clear directions about what is acceptable behavior. When kids only know what not to do and not what they should be doing, they're more likely to break rules because they don't have anywhere to direct their energy.

Instead of coming up with a list of 'don'ts,' try to give your kids instructions on what behavior is expected of them. If one of your rules is "don't watch TV an hour before bedtime," you can revise it to say "start winding down an hour before bedtime." You might give them calming activities like reading or coloring to keep them occupied without making them hyper before they need to go to bed. If you would normally tell your child "don't leave your toys out around the house," try telling them to pick up after themselves when they're done playing. Instead of "don't yell," you can say "speak softly," and instead of "don't hit," you can say "take deep breaths when you're mad and keep your hands to yourself." The action you want them to take is the same, but the way you ask makes all the difference. It gives your child a way to comply without their feeling reprimanded. Using 'dos' instead of 'don'ts' also helps kids feel like they're doing the right thing. They feel good about themselves for doing what you want and you can praise them for good behavior, which is something that is harder to do if they're only told not to do something.

Talk With Your Child, Not at Them

A conversation requires two active participants. If one person is talking "at" the other, not allowing them to get a word in edgewise and disregarding their opinions, this is a lecture, not a conversation. It's important to invite your child to talk with you rather than simply talking at them. Ask them to be part of the conversation too. If you talk "at" your child, you might look outside at a stormy sky and say, "put your raincoat on." Your child might resist simply because they feel like they don't have a choice. Instead of having a one-sided conversation, you could say, "Look at the sky. What do you think the weather is going to be? If it rains, how are you going to keep yourself dry?" This involves them in the decision, rather than separating them from it. .

Talking with our kids reinforces the idea that their opinions are valuable and allows them to express some agency. If we disregard this and talk at a child, we give the message that their thoughts and feelings are not important or interesting, and that the parenting relationship is about the child doing what *you* want" (van der Linden, n.d., para. 16). Ideally, the relationship should be about the two of you supporting the growth and development of your child.

Kids should be able to give input when appropriate, and they should know why they have to act a certain way if it's a non-negotiable issue. When you sit down and talk to and with your child rather than at them, you show them you want them to understand not just what the rules are but why they're important. You invite them to give feedback about which rules are difficult for them to follow and why that might be the case so you can address any problems they might be having, resulting in better behavior and communication.

Use 'I' Statements

Kids need to understand how their actions and words impact the people around them. They tend to take a self-centered view, in part because they are still developing the parts of their minds that allow them to see things from someone else's point of view. We can help them get into the habit of considering the consequences of their actions by using 'I' statements. These are statements that show things from our first-person perspective and help us communicate our feelings or thoughts.

The most common type of 'I' statement is the "I feel" statement. This helps us explain our emotions in a non-confrontational way. If our kids are constantly demanding our attention when we're tired or distracted, we might say, "You're being annoying." This can make kids feel upset, especially if they didn't realize the effect their actions were having on us. Instead, we can say, "I feel too tired to play with you right now," or "I feel frustrated when you don't listen to me." If our kids say something mean to us when we discipline them—something intentionally hurtful like "I hate you"—we can resist the urge to respond with something we might regret and instead say, "I feel upset when you talk to me that way." This is a more neutral way to state the problem that still helps kids recognize the role they play. Our kids will then feel more inclined to change their behaviors because they understand the way these behaviors are hurting us.

There are other kinds of 'I' statements that can help you get your point across. With 'I' statements, "Your room is messy" becomes "I would like you to clean your room." "Stop crying" becomes "I need you to calm down and talk to me so I can understand what the problem is." Often, 'I' statements are what we really mean to say in these situations once we calm down and discard our immediate emotional response. They are more productive for problem solving and they encourage kids to start considering how their actions make others feel. This is a skill that every child needs to learn at some point in their lives in order to have healthy social relationships.

Make Your Requests Important

While it's important to show our kids the same respect we'd like to be shown, we also have to remember that ultimately, we're the ones in charge. If we are too passive in our requests, we risk being ignored. This can make us frustrated and lead to us lashing out at our kids. When we ask them to do something, we need to let them know that we expect them to do it. If we use passive language like "Could you please take off your shoes when you've been out in the mud" or "Would you like to wash your hands before dinner?" we are more likely to be ignored or rejected, especially if our kids are already doing an activity that they find more fun than the one we're trying to get them to do.

Be direct with your words, and if your child resists doing the task, give them a reason why it's important they get it done now other than "because I said so." For example, if you want them to help set the dinner table, you might say "please help me set out the plates for dinner. If you do, we can eat soon." Let them know why you want them to act so they can see why agreeing is in their best interest. You are still making a request, but you're not asking a question they can say no to in most circumstances.

As your child gets older, you likely won't need to be as strict in your requests. Once they understand why a given task is important, they will put up less resistance. They may also have responsibilities that keep them from being able to follow your instructions right away. For example, they might have a lot of homework they need to get done, so they can't clean their room as soon as you ask them. If this happens, ask them when they'll be able to do it and hold them to their promise. This compromise shows mutual respect while still telling your child that they need to listen when you ask them to do something.

Use Kind Words

Many parents say mean and judgmental things to their kids, often without thinking through what they're saying. They might tell their kids, "You're acting like a baby," or, "You're being a brat." What they really mean to say is that the kids' behavior is unacceptable, but because the parent used unkind words the message gets muddled. It becomes a personal attack rather than an attempt to get kids to listen and correct their behavior.

These cruel words typically come more from a place of frustration than anything else, and while they might not be meant to be harmful, that doesn't change their hurtful effect. Just imagine if your boss came up to you and started speaking to you in the same tone you use with your child.

Imagine if they constantly criticized you and your efforts, especially if you didn't fully understand what they wanted you to do. You would be upset, angry, and resentful, and it might impact your ability to listen to your boss in the future. You might purposefully do things you know you aren't supposed to in an effort to get back at them. In short, you wouldn't feel very cooperative at all.

Our kids react in much the same way when we are unkind to them. They may also develop issues with their self-image and self-esteem if we repeatedly criticize them. We may not even recognize the harm we're doing until down the road. The best way to avoid this problem is to shift the language we use to talk to our kids. Be more considerate toward your child and accept that they will make some mistakes. Differentiate between bad behaviors they do because they're being malicious and bad behaviors that are accidents, or ones that only occurred because they didn't know any better. If your child breaks something accidentally, this should be treated differently than if they smashed something out of spite. Instead of punishment, practice kindness and forgiveness. This teaches kids that it's okay to make mistakes and that they can come to you with problems without fearing they'll be yelled at for an accident. Building this trusting and accepting relationship early on is crucial for navigating the more chaotic teenage years. Let your child know that no matter what they do, you'll always love them, and never resort to name-calling or other harsh criticism.

Make sure to praise kids when they do something well too. If they are playing nicely with another child, let them know they're doing the right thing. If they take the initiative to help with clean-up, be sure to thank them. This reinforces good behaviors, which can be even more powerful than discouraging bad ones. Kids feel good when you praise them, which creates a positive feedback loop that results in better behavior. Again, we want to reward the effort, not necessarily the result. Instead of saying, "I'm proud of you for getting an A on your test," we can say, "I'm proud of all the studying you did." This tells kids that good behavior matters more than any grade ever could, and it also reminds them that you'll love them regardless of how well they do in school. If your child studies hard and gives a test their all only to get a bad grade, they shouldn't have to worry about your reaction. Instead, they can bring you their test grade right away.

PHRASES FOR WHEN KIDS AREN'T LISTENING

When our kids aren't listening to us, our first reaction is typically anger and frustration. At this point, we are arguing, not talking to each other or listening to what the other person has to say. This impedes good behavior and turns an opportunity for education into a cacophony of tears, yelling, and hurt feelings.

If your child is refusing to listen to you, there is a wall standing in the way of good communication. Breaking down this wall is important for reestablishing trust and under-standing. However, if we try to forcefully knock the wall down by yelling, pulling, or hitting, we do more harm than good. Instead, we must stay calm, reassess the situation, and redirect our kids so they listen to us again. To accomplish this, we can use different phrases that help dispel tension and better understand each other. If they're ignoring us, we can say, "I feel upset when you don't listen to me." If they are starting to yell, asking them to "lower your volume" is more effective than yelling right back. These phrases can turn an emotionally charged situation into a learning opportunity. It is only through this process of clearing the air, de-escalating the conflict, and bringing kids' attention back to ourselves that we can get kids to communicate with us and listen to us once again.

Use Your Inside Voice

Parents aren't the only ones who are tempted to yell when something's going wrong. Kids can get worked up too, and they might scream or wail if they're not getting their way. This is never a productive way to have a conversation. When a child is yelling, they're not ready to listen. But if we tell kids to "be quiet" or "shut up," we're telling them not to make noise at all. We're silencing them and telling them we don't care what they have to say. This usually isn't something they could do even if they wanted to.

Instead, try telling upset kids who raise their voices, "Use your inside voice." This tells your child a few things. The first is that the current volume of their voice is unacceptable and it needs to change. The second is that you're not going to be able to listen to what they're trying to tell you unless they lower their voices.

Finally, this phrase also tells kids that you do want to hear their point of view. You are interested in what they have to say; you just don't want to hear it at 90 decibels. When you put things this way, kids see lowering their voice as a step toward getting you to listen to rather than ignore them. It becomes something they want to do because they know the outcome will be positive for them, with the added benefit of being positive for you too.

Do You Want Help?

We often try to rush in to help our kids, and fix whatever is wrong right away. If our kids are attempting to tie their shoelaces and getting upset when they can't do it, we might demand they just give the shoe to us so we can finally leave the house. When we do this, we take the agency out of our kids' hands. We tell them they're not good enough to do it themselves, and we take away their ability to improve their motor skills. We risk making them more upset because they see their attempt as ending in failure.

Rather than grabbing the reins right away, try asking your child, "Do you want some help with that?" This puts the ball in their court. They can choose to ask you for help or continue to work at their task and figure it out for themselves. The important thing to remember if you ask your child if they want help is to listen to the answer they give. If they say no and you immediately disregard it, they're not going to feel like they have any control. Let them ask you for help before you take over.

Use Your Teamwork Skills

As your child learns new social skills, help them give a name to these skills. When they play nicely with a sibling or classmate and they take turns being in charge of the game, let them know that these are teamwork skills. When they make an effort to listen quietly and attentively when you're talking to them, praise them for their listening skills. By naming these skills, you encourage your child to keep practicing them. You can also remind your child of these skill sets when they forget to use them.

When you're correcting your child, use positive language. If you notice your child is playing with friends and they're always the one in charge, you might be tempted to tell them no one will want to play with them if they're bossy. This kind of negative language tells your child what they're doing is wrong but doesn't help them fix the problem. It just makes them feel bad about their actions. If you wanted to give this a more positive spin, you might tell them to use their team-work or listening skills. This reminds them that others might want to decide what game they're playing—without making your child feel bad for the way they acted. It is a gentle encouragement to alter their behavior.

The type of skills you suggest depends on the situation. If you need them to settle down and concentrate on one assignment, you might ask them to use their focusing skills. In other scenarios, problem-solving or critical-thinking skills might be more appropriate.

It's Okay to Be Upset

Young kids have trouble compartmentalizing their feelings. A small problem can feel like a colossal issue, even if it can be fixed very easily. As an adult, you know there's no use crying over the small stuff in life, but kids typically don't have this awareness. Something as minor as their favorite show not being on or being asked to wear their red sneakers instead of their blue ones can lead to a total meltdown.

In these cases, we might be tempted to tell kids to stop crying or remind them that the source of their anger or sadness isn't a big deal. Rather than getting kids to stop crying, this usually only makes things worse. When we tell our kids to "get over it," we are invalidating the way they feel. It may not seem like a big deal to us, but to them the issue clearly matters a lot. Additionally, telling kids to ignore their feelings can actually make it harder for them to manage their emotions. They may have trouble recognizing their feelings and may not know how to handle it when they can't keep the feeling at bay any longer. To be more considerate of their feelings and promote healthy emotional growth, we can tell our kids it's okay to be upset when things go wrong. It's not weak to be afraid of something, and crying isn't for babies. These emotions are natural, and no child should be discouraged from feeling them.

That being said, the way kids express their emotions can often leave something to be desired. It's fine for your child to cry when they are hurt or afraid, but it's not okay for them to scream, break things, or hit people. Let your child know that while it's okay to feel sad or angry, it's not okay to express their sadness or anger in destructive ways. You can offer alternative methods for dealing with these feelings, like letting them spend some time alone to calm down, or getting them to take a few deep breaths.

The next time your child starts tearing up about something like their favorite show not being on TV, start off by reminding them that it's okay for them to feel sad or angry if they were expecting one thing but got another. Remember that a change in the TV station's programming is a big deal to your child, even if it doesn't seem like much of an issue to you. If they're being destructive, follow this up by saying it's not okay to act that way just because they're upset.

Finally, redirect that anger and sadness into something more productive. Ask them if they'd like to burn off some steam by going for a walk instead of watching TV, or if they'd rather have some alone time.

Put It on Your Birthday List

Just about every parent has been there before: you're in the store trying to buy only what's necessary, and your child races to grab some toy or game off the shelf. You don't want to add an unnecessary surprise purchase to your bill, especially if you're tight on cash this week, but you also know the meltdown that's coming if you say no. What should you do?

The best solution here is usually one that involves delayed gratification. This is the idea that when we wait for something good to happen and we feel like we've worked for it rather than accepting something that was just handed to us, we enjoy it more. Delayed gratification is also a good way for kids to practice self-control. You can tell your child that you can't get the toy or game right now, but if they behave themselves maybe you can get it for them for their birthday, or another closer holiday. Ask them to write it down on their birthday list, or write the list for them if they're too young to do it themselves. When their birthday comes around, they can pick toys they still want to get. This keeps you from buying toys your child will get tired of within a week, and it also encourages your child to be on their best behavior so they can get their reward. When they unwrap their toy, they'll know they got it because of their good communication and listening skills, not because they threw a tantrum in the middle of the store when you said no.

Let's Try That Again

Kids may need to try things a few times before they get it right. This is true for most skills they learn like reading, writing, and dressing themselves, but it's also true for social situations. Maybe you planned a fun trip for the family, but arguments broke out. Maybe your child was trying to show you something they learned but they didn't get it right and they got upset instead. Maybe you tried to deal with your child's fussing and you ended up handling it the wrong way. In these situations, the best thing you can do is suggest a do-over.

If a fun activity or a conversation goes the wrong way, try starting over again. Take it from the top, but this time remember to keep calm and avoid the mistakes of last time. Adjust how you handle a tricky situation so everyone has more fun this time around. Let your child make a few attempts until they have a better handle on their words or actions. A second chance gives everyone the opportunity to recognize how things went wrong before and make sure they don't go wrong in the same way again.

Let's say you wanted to have a family trip to the park, but before you even got out the door you got in an argument with your child. Maybe they started arguing with you about what outfit they wanted to wear. If you don't patch things up, the argument can sour the whole trip. Give everyone a moment to calm down, then ask your child if they'd like to try that again. This time, when you start getting them dressed, try to be more receptive to their opinions and remain calm when you explain why they can't wear a heavy outfit when it's very hot outside. Maybe take them outside so they can feel the temperature for themselves, which will help them realize why your instructions make sense. This is the same scenario again, but this time without all the arguing and hurt feelings. Now you're starting the trip on a positive note.

What Did You Learn?

Every difficult situation is an opportunity for kids to learn something. There is always some new lesson to learn when we go through hardship. We might learn something about ourselves, about how we should act in certain situations, or about other people. If your child experiences an upsetting situation, turning it into something they can learn from is a great way to make the experience a little more positive in their mind. This can ease some of the sting of the situation. Even though it was hard to experience, it was also a necessary experience that taught them more about themselves and the world around them.

As an example, let's say your child had an argument with their sibling. Instead of handling the argument respectfully, they hit their sibling. Your child will probably get upset if you point out how this behavior is unacceptable. If you send them to time out and they're still angry, try asking them, "Do you know why what you did wasn't okay? What did you learn from this?" The lesson here should be that hitting is wrong, and it's better to use your words during an argument. When you reframe the situation this way, your child understands why they're facing consequences for their actions. They also have an easier time remembering the lesson next time they have the urge to hit someone when they're mad.

What Do You Think You Can Do?

If your child makes a mistake, your first instinct might be to fix the mistake for them. If they upset their sibling or a friend, you might try to smooth over the situation yourself. If they got reprimanded for their behavior at school, you might call up their teacher and direct your anger at them. When we take over situations for our kids, we don't help them as much as we think we do. We take away control of the situation, and we diminish the consequences of their actions.

Instead of fixing things ourselves, we can ask our kids what they think they can do to fix the situation. If they made their sibling cry, ask them what they can do to cheer them up. You can suggest an apology if they have trouble arriving at an answer, but let them decide.

Additionally, use this as a chance to reinforce consequences. If they knocked over their toys to purposefully make a mess, let them know the consequence of their actions is to pick up their toys without your help. This will teach them not to repeat the behavior, as they know they will have to work harder to fix it than if you had cleaned up the toys yourself.

I'm Here to Support You

No matter what our kids do, they will always be our kids. We don't want to rescue our kids from situations created by their bad behavior, but we do want to support them when they try to make things right and fix their mistakes. We can let them know we care and want them to succeed. We can remind them we love them all the time so they never doubt it for a moment, even if they make us very mad. When our kids know we're in their corner, they're more likely to listen to us and come to us for guidance with their problems.

As you continue to reinforce good behaviors and discourage bad ones in non-confrontational ways, your child will learn everything they need to know to have a healthy relationship with you and other people in their lives. By encouraging communication and responsiveness, you do so much more than just talk. You are laying the foundation for their future development.

6

THE ONE VITAL SKILL YOUR KIDS MIGHT BE STRUGGLING WITH AND HOW TO FIX IT !

O f the many skills kids learn when they are still developing, communication is perhaps the most important. Without good communication skills, kids can have trouble relating to their peers. They may struggle to form significant relationships both inside and outside the family. They may argue with you more often, and they can engage in more bad behavior because they don't know any other way to make themselves heard. They see all attention as good attention, even if it means they have to draw attention to themselves by being loud, rude, or disobedient. It's possible they will find it harder to learn when they're at school, as "a child who is good at communicating verbally will find it easier to produce written communications, and thus will likely perform better in their school exams and written assignments" (Kumon, 2016, para. 8).

Despite this, many kids struggle to communicate their desires effectively, simply because they haven't been taught the right way to talk to others. They may struggle to explain how they feel in productive ways, or they may be held back by extreme shyness that prevents them from making friends. If these issues are not corrected in early childhood, they can pose problems for many years. Some communication issues can even follow kids into their teenage, young adult, and adult years. Shyness can develop into anxiety, a commanding or bossy personality can drive away potential friends and impede their social development, and trouble with school could hurt their ability to get into a good college and secure a job. These issues are very far into the future, of course, so you still have plenty of time to make sure your child has the skills they need to avoid them when they grow up. Right now, you can have the greatest impact on your child's future success by teaching them good communication skills.

WHY KIDS STRUGGLE WITH EFFECTIVE COMMUNICATION

Difficulties with communication can make themselves known in a few different ways. Kids who struggle to communicate effectively often try to make their feelings and opinions known another way, mainly through making a fuss and throwing temper tantrums. They don't know how to talk about their wants and needs with their words, so they resort to drawing attention to themselves and demanding what they want. A child who exhibits these behaviors may only be doing so because they don't have the tools for more rational self-expression.

On the other hand, some kids may be too timid to reach out and socialize with people they're unfamiliar with. They might come alive in the home, but as soon as they leave the house, they completely clam up. You might not consider this shyness to be a big deal at first—after all, it's less disruptive than kids who run around and shriek at the top of their lungs in public places—but it can be an indicator that your child is having difficulties communicating. They may have experience being misheard or misunderstood by others, so they have stopped making attempts to communicate. They may be frightened of strangers, or they may have difficulty being honest and open with people when they speak. Any of these issues could point to difficulties with communication.

As much as we might like one clear reason for communication issues, the real answer to why our kids might have trouble communicating effectively isn't so cut and dried. It may be a combination of reasons, each stemming from a social or developmental source. Previous experiences can contribute to how a child expresses themselves. Sometimes, kids just need a little more time to figure themselves out and get their mood swings under control. However, if these issues persist long past when kids should have grown out of them, it's time to take a closer look at your child's behavior. Consider the different factors that could be contributing to their communication difficulties and try to identify whether each one of the following potential sources applies to your child.

A Lack of Guidance

Parenting in the modern world can be very difficult because of how busy we are all the time. Most households can't afford to have one parent stay home with their child all day, which means other childcare solutions become necessary. A child could end up spending more time at daycare, where they are one face among a dozen or more kids, than they do with their parents at home. When we get home from work, we may be so tired that we struggle to give our kids the attention they need for their development. We're more likely to sit them down in front of the TV or let them play on a phone or tablet than we are to still have the energy required for spending quality time with our kids. This parenting style and the increased amount of time kids spend in front of a screen can contribute to difficulties forming human connections. If kids don't get enough practice talking with us, their communication skills can suffer.

Similar issues can arise if we unknowingly set a bad example for our kids. If we argue with our spouse and raise our voices, our kids may overhear this and learn that this is how adults talk to each other. They may come to believe that this is the way they should communicate too, even if we tell them otherwise. Kids learn by seeing, and if all they see are bad examples they will pick up and internalize this behavior.

We can alleviate some of these difficulties by making sure we carve out a little time each day to spend with our kids. This might be during mealtimes, bathtimes, or before bed if we have a busy schedule. Additionally, any time we get to spend with our kids should be spent paying attention to them. If we get distracted with the television or with our phone, we're not giving our kids the attention and feedback they need to develop their social skills.

Trouble With Social Cues

Some kids may have trouble communicating because they don't know how to pick up on social cues. These are the small facial movements and posture changes that tip us off to how other people feel without needing to hear them say it out loud. Kids who aren't great communicators may have trouble "reading a room." They might tell a joke at an inappropriate time, interrupt their conversation partners, or keep a conversation going long after it's clear the other person wants it to end. The social cues that give us this information are recognized so automatically by our brains that we hardly have to think about them, but some kids may not be as adept at picking up these cues as most adults. They can unknowingly make conversations unpleasant or make others feel awkward, which might drive potential friends away and limit their opportunities to socialize.

Some kids just aren't as interested in socializing. This isn't necessarily a bad thing but does mean these kids don't get as much practice reading facial cues and body language as their peers. They can fall behind because of a lack of practice, which makes it harder for them to catch back up.

Not Paying Attention

Lots of kids have trouble participating in the typical flow of a conversation because they're not paying attention. Their thoughts may be elsewhere, or they may be so excited by what they want to say that they forget to listen. Kids who are easily distracted and have difficulty listening may be more likely to interrupt in the middle of someone else's sentence, or they may say something that seems like a total non-sequitur to whatever they were saying before. If you find that you frequently have to ask your child what they mean by what they said, this may be a problem with their language skills.

Similar difficulties that can plague easily distracted kids is proper word choice. They can get their vocabulary jumbled up, or they may spend a long time trying to come up with the word they want to use. When they remember it, they blurt it out, regardless of whether the conversation has moved on in the meantime. Without being able to focus on the conversation at hand, overactive thoughts can become a barrier to natural conversation.

Impulsivity and Anxiety

Impulsive behaviors are those that aren't fully thought through before we act on them. If we act impulsively, we might say or do something we don't mean or we might perform these behaviors without considering how they might affect other people. Kids who struggle with acting impulsively might find it difficult to reign in their gut responses to situations. They may say something they don't know is rude but still has the power to hurt someone's feelings. They might speak as soon as they come up with something to say rather than waiting for a pause in the conversation. They might also get angry if they feel they're not being listened to, even if they're not making an effort to listen to others.

Kids who feel anxious are more likely to act impulsively. They may do or say things that make the conversation awkward for both parties. This can discourage them from participating in the conversation and make their worries worse. They might see their conversational faux-pas as a much more serious event than the simple, fixable mistake it was thanks to their anxiety. They may then act on an impulse to retreat from the conversation, which can keep them from getting the necessary practice to overcome their fears. Impulsiveness and anxiety go hand in hand, and they can each make the other one worse if nothing is done to help your child improve their communication skills.

Communication Disorders

On top of the previous reasons, it is also possible that your child may have a communication disorder that is restricting their ability to hold a conversation. They may have a shortened attention span because of attention deficit hyperactivity disorder (ADHD), or they may have a developmental issue that makes it harder for them to process and communicate their feelings. Kids may also have trouble feeling heard if they have a speech impediment, which can make it harder for others to understand them. If you suspect your child has any of these issues, seek out a specialist for a professional diagnosis. Defer to any recommended treatment plan and ask what you can do to help.

Whatever the reason for your child's difficulties getting their point across, understanding where the issue stems from can help you more effectively address it. If you know your child is having trouble picking up on body language cues, you can practice more activities that involve reading body language. If you believe a communication disorder could be holding them back, you can speak to a specialist. Knowing the underlying issue allows you to take more effective steps to address the problem and improve your child's communication skills.

METHODS FOR IMPROVING COMMUNICATION SKILLS

If your child struggles with communicating, there are plenty of opportunities for you to help them improve their skills. No child is destined to be a bad communicator forever. With some assistance from you, any child can learn to improve their social awareness and their ability to engage in conversation. With these activities, exercises, and everyday practices, you can teach your child more about why communication matters and how they can get better.

Encourage Active Listening

Previously, we mentioned the value of practicing active listening with your child. When you listen actively, you take an interest in what they have to say by nodding your head, offering encouragement or interest, and adding to the conversation without interrupting. Now, we'll take a look at how you can encourage your child to model the same behaviors.

Part of encouraging active listening is demonstrating the behavior yourself. Show your child how it's done before you ask them to try it. Then you can explain to them how to listen actively, and they'll understand how good it feels to know the other person is listening. In conversations, gently encourage them to make eye contact and check in every so often to make sure they're listening. Eventually, they will pick up the active listening behaviors.

As always, listening is an integral part of communication. When kids start actively listening, they're more likely to absorb what they are hearing and pick up on social cues. They'll get a feeling for the natural flow of conversation, and because they're listening actively, they'll be able to respond in an appropriate way.

Expand Your Child's Vocabulary

Difficulties in communicating can arise because kids lack the words they need to express themselves. They may work themselves up with no way to explain how they're feeling other than to cry or yell. We can assist our kids by teaching them to explain their feelings and make themselves understood. The larger your child's vocabulary is, the easier it will be for them to express themselves, and the less they will have to rely on more dramatic outbursts.

There are many different ways you can teach your young child new words. One method is to name emotions as your child experiences them. If you can see them getting red in the face and clenching their fists, let them know they're feeling angry. If they start to tear up, name the emotion as sadness or frustration. Assist them in figuring out the right name for whatever they feel.

Reading is another great way to teach your child new words. When you read together, you can explain any unfamiliar words they might come across. Kids who read more develop a larger vocabulary, which often translates to more confidence in their communication skills. They also tend to have an easier time talking about themselves, and they may even find it easier to identify how others are feeling because they learn to empathize with the characters in their books.

Don't be afraid to use words your child might not know in conversations with them. Many parents simplify their language when talking to their kids, but this ensures the kids won't learn anything new from the conversation. Use more complex words as you would when talking to an adult, and let your child know it's okay to ask for clarification. Sometimes kids can figure out meanings from context clues, but other times they will need explanation. Make sure not to judge them for any words they might not know, as this could discourage them from asking for help in the future.

If you hear your child using a word incorrectly, try to gently correct them. You don't want to overcorrect to the point that you're nitpicking or constantly correcting them, but you also don't want to let them continue using the word incorrectly. This could lead to greater confusion in conversations.

Remain patient with your child, and if you don't understand what they're trying to say, ask them what they mean until you have a good idea of the word they intended to use.

Pay Attention to Your Body Language

Just like active listening, it's easier to teach kids about body language when we demonstrate it for them first. When you're speaking to your child, make an effort to ensure your body language matches what you're trying to say. Keep your posture relaxed and open when you're happy. If you're feeling tense and stressed, let your body reflect this too. The more kids see different kinds of body language, the better they'll become at identifying the emotion behind the body language and picking up on cues they would have otherwise missed.

You can also directly teach your child about body language. Take the opportunity to point out different body language in pictures and TV shows you watch together. You can even mention the body language of other kids your child is interacting with. If another child has their arms crossed and they're avoiding eye contact, explain that this might mean they're nervous or uncomfortable. Ask your child about what they think they could do to help them feel more comfortable and what kind of behaviors would be inappropriate for the situation. Eventually, they will be able to determine the best approach without needing your guidance.

Involve Their Imagination

Kids learn a lot from playing pretend. If you want to help them improve their communication skills, trying role playing some situations they might encounter in their lives with them. Pretend you're another child on the playground and let your child pretend they're meeting you for the first time. You can guide them through a conversation that will help them make a new friend, which lets them feel more comfortable when the situation presents itself in real life. The practice kids get from trying things out in a safe, low-stakes environment is incredibly helpful.

It can also be useful to encourage kids to talk about their emotions by creating stories with their toys. If your child is in an argument with one of their friends, they might find it tough to talk about it with you. They might feel more comfortable playing a game where their stuffed animal was having the same trouble with their friend. It is often easier to say their toy is scared and upset than it is for them to use the same labels to describe themselves. As you show your child how the stuffed animal resolves their conflict, he or she learns to apply the same methods to the conflict in their life.

Talk Frequently

The best way to improve communication is through prac-tice. If kids don't talk, they'll find it harder to develop effective communication skills. If they get the practice they need through conversations with you, they'll be able to use the same skills to talk to just about anyone. Take every opportunity to talk to your child about their day, their feelings, and their opinions. Encourage them to open up but don't be afraid to have a casual conversation either. Talk when you're doing an activity together or when you're just spending time with each other around the house. The simple act of talking is powerful. Your child will feel more comfortable communicating, and they will continue improving these invaluable skills.

PHRASES TO ENCOURAGE MEANINGFUL CONVERSATIONS

Just as we looked at phrases we can use when kids aren't listening, we will also look at phrases we can use to get our kids to open up and talk about topics that are important to them. These phrases are deceptively simple. They can often open the floodgates and get your child to really start talking about what interests them.

What Are You Looking Forward To?

Kids' schedules are usually fairly busy. They probably have playdates with friends, extracurricular activities, and family events in their near future. They might even have a birthday party or two to attend.

There is a lot for kids to look forward to. If you know there's something fun coming up for your child, ask them about it. Ask what they're excited about and what they plan to do that day. This is a natural topic of conversation for kids to latch onto because it's inherently interesting to them. This can help coax quiet or gloomy kids out of their shells, as even the shyest child has interests and fun hobbies they would be happy to discuss with you. It also helps you learn a little more about what your child finds fun and what kinds of activities are exciting to them.

What Kind of Superpower Would You Like to Have?

This is a classic question for all ages. If you're looking for a good conversation topic, ask your child what superpower they would most like to have and why. Would they like to soar over crowds, or would they like to rewind time and undo a bad decision? Maybe they'd like to be super strong, or perhaps they're more interested in invisibility. Whatever answer you get, it's sure to be a fun topic, and it can reveal areas your child might like a little extra help in. For example, reading minds might be more appealing if your child thinks it could help them better understand what other people want them to say. This answer might indicate your child is having difficulties with their listening or memory skills, or that they haven't yet mastered some of the social norms for conversations and they tend to talk out of turn. You can then address these issues with practice and other exercises.

When Did You Feel Happiest Today?

All too often, we find ourselves asking kids to talk about tough emotions like anger and sadness. We want them to explain these feelings, but we rarely pay as much attention to more positive feelings. If we focus too heavily on all the negative parts of life, it might even feel like these emotions are the only ones we ever experience.

Flip this on its head and ask your child about when they felt happiest during the day. They'll speak more enthusiastically, and they'll naturally practice gratitude for the good things in their life rather than dwelling on the difficult moments.

7

NOW LET'S MAKE LEARNING FUN!

Improving communication with your child doesn't have to be all work. You can involve some play in your strategy as well. In fact, making learning fun is one of the best ways to engage your child. It captures your child's attention and helps them feel like they're part of the lesson rather than feeling like they're being lectured at. Using exercises and games allows your child to take part in their own education and gives them an opportunity to practice their skills. It also takes some of the pressure off of getting things right. They have time and space to make a mistake or lose their temper without hurting someone's feelings. When an opportunity to use these skills for real comes around, they will be ready to nail it.

GAMES AND ACTIVITIES FOR COMMUNICATION

The exercises included in this chapter help kids practice different aspects of good communication. These include conversation skills, emotional maturity, empathy, being respectful, and taking turns speaking. Kids are encouraged to identify their feelings in different situations, talk about themselves, and listen to what others have to say. These activities are a great addition to any household game night or lesson plan.

Show and Tell

In show and tell, each participant selects an item that is personally valuable to them. When it's their turn, the child will get up in front of the room and show everyone their object. Then they will explain why they picked it and why. Once they're finished presenting, the other participants can ask questions about the item. You can make show and tell extra fun by giving kids a specific theme for their item. For example, one week you might ask everyone to bring a book they enjoy. The next week, you might ask them to bring a drawing they made. This helps keep things interesting and gives kids some guidance on what makes the item important to them.

Show and tell gives kids practice with public speaking, as they're giving a presentation to family or peers. They get to present in a safe environment where there is no one trying to discourage or mock them. Everyone is giving them their attention, which can help them feel heard and valued. Through show and tell, kids learn how to describe an object to another person. They also learn how to tell a story if they share something that happened to them that involved the item they're presenting. When the rest of the group asks questions about their item, they get practice coming up with answers on the spot. Once they're done presenting, they also get to exercise their listening skills by watching others present and asking their own relevant questions.

Telephone

To play telephone, have everyone sit close to each other in a circle. Designate one person, typically the oldest player, to be the start of the telephone. The starter comes up with a word or short phrase. Then they whisper that phrase in the ear of the person sitting next to them. That person whispers what they heard to the next person, and so on until the message reaches the beginning of the telephone again. Starting with the first person, have everyone say aloud what message they think they heard from the last person. While you might assume everyone will say the same thing, there is usually at least one point where someone mishears or speaks too softly for the next person to get the right message, which means there was a small, often silly miscommunication. The game is most fun when played with many people, as the chances increase that the message will get jumbled as it makes its way around the circle.

The telephone game teaches kids about the way a message can be misheard or misunderstood as it moves from person to person. If they whispered the phrase "tiny cat," the person next to them might have heard them say "shiny rat." Even though neither of them were trying to get the message wrong on purpose, the miscommunication still happened.

This teaches kids to be careful with their words and anticipate that sometimes what we hear people say isn't actually what they meant. This can get them to be more forgiving of miscommunications in the future. It can also help them speak clearly so they have a better chance of being understood and avoiding a miscommunication altogether.

Finish the Story

"Finish the story" is a collaborative game for everyone in the family or class to work together to create one complete story. To play, start with a simple, open-ended introduction, such as, "there was a big brown dog who..." Once you start the story, let the next person continue where you left off. Each person should add a line or two to the story, with no one person contributing too much or too little. Once you've gone around the room a few times, you will have created a story that is entirely unique and shared by everyone.

This game teaches kids to cooperate with others. It teaches them collaboration while also letting them showcase their storytelling skills. The game also asks kids to listen to everyone else when they're talking, or they won't know what to do when it's their turn to add to the story. Taking turns is another valuable lesson the game can teach. Instead of telling the entire story themselves, kids must take turns with everyone else and let them contribute. Each of these lessons is integral to good communication.

Playing Pretend

Playing pretend probably isn't something you have to introduce to your child, as kids tend to pick this one up naturally. They want to mimic the behaviors they see other people do, and they want to let their imaginations run wild. When kids play pretend, they act like someone else for a little while. This could mean they pretend to do what you do, or it could mean they imagine what it would be like to be an astronaut, an explorer, or another dream job.

Aside from its benefits for creativity, playing pretend also lets kids improve communication skills. When kids play pretend as a group, they get used to the idea of designating and fulfilling roles as part of a team. For example, in a group of kids who play house, kids typically decide who will be the mommy, the daddy, the brothers and sisters, and other members of the family. Then they act out those roles and relationships with the other kids. They learn that teamwork often means each person does a slightly different role, even though they're all working toward the same goal. Playing pretend is also great for your child's ability to put themselves in someone else's shoes. This is a great exercise that helps them understand and accommodate other peoples' perspectives.

Emotional Charades

In a typical game of charades, players must act out a word or phrase completely nonverbally. They can only pantomime and try to get their message across without talking. Other players will then try to guess what word the person is miming. In emotional charades, all of the phrases being acted out are different emotions.

To play, write down a list of emotions or situations that might cause an emotional reaction. These might include simple emotions like happy and sad, more complex feelings like loneliness and frustration, or emotional situations like losing something important or getting a new toy. Each word or phrase should be on its own piece of paper. Put all the papers in a bowl and have one player draw a paper. They must act out whatever they see.

Emotional charades helps kids pick up on methods of communication other than talking. They connect different facial expressions and body language to their corresponding emotions as they're acting, and they learn to pick up on these nonverbal cues when they're guessing. This can help them gain a better understanding of their feelings. This is especially true if the phrases everyone is acting out are emotional situations. Through charades, kids learn what they should expect to feel in different situations, which can better prepare them to experience these situations in real life.

Simon Says

Simon says is a game where one person is designated as the leader, or "Simon." Simon then asks the other players to perform different simple tasks, but players should only do tasks that are preceded by the phrase "Simon Says." If a player does a task but Simon didn't use the phrase, they are eliminated from the game.

Simon says tests kids' ability to listen and pay attention. Kids will be focused on whoever is chosen to be Simon because they have to listen to whether or not they say "Simon says."

Winning the game involves carefully listening to what someone else is saying. The game also encourages kids to follow instructions, as they need to in order to play. This creates a mental connection between listening to instructions and having fun. The game can even be used to get kids to do simple chores around the house. For example, some of the tasks you say as Simon might include "Simon says put one of your toys in the bin" or "Simon says pick out a snack for your lunchbox." The games are quick and can be played for only a few rounds if you just want to make cleanup time a little more fun.

Twenty Questions

In Twenty Questions, one player mentally chooses an item that is somewhere in the room. Once they've secretly chosen their item, the other players take turns trying to guess which item they chose by asking a series of yes or no questions. The person answering the questions can only say "yes," "no," "maybe," or "sometimes." After the guessers have asked their combined 20 questions, they attempt to figure out what item the first player is thinking about.

Twenty questions teaches kids to observe and describe their surroundings. They identify key traits about the object they select such as its size, shape, and color, all of which might be questions they need to answer. When kids are guessing instead of answering questions, they learn to consider their words carefully, as they need to figure out which item is the right one without using all 20 questions. They ask more insightful, specific questions that are more likely to give them a better idea of what kind of item they should be looking for. They also learn that closed-ended questions, or those that can be answered by a simple "yes" or "no," are not always the most helpful. They understand that responding to questions with brief answers and minimal explanation can be frustrating for the person asking the question, so they're more likely to ask open-ended questions and give more information in their answers next time.

Board Games

There are many board games that improve kids' communication skills. Each of these games can be used to reinforce communication skills. While they may seem like mindless fun, they're actually teaching valuable lessons.

Classics like *Scrabble* let them practice their spelling skills and can expand their vocabulary. Games like *Battleship* or *Clue* require kids to pay attention and listen to other players' answers to have the best chance at winning. *Guess Who* teaches kids to ask specific questions, and to observe and describe different physical attributes. The various activities in *Cranium* encourage players to communicate in a variety of different verbal and nonverbal ways.

Aside from these specific examples, playing games as a family is a great way to bond and improve communication skills. You're using critical-thinking and problem-solving skills to play games, and you're enjoying your shared time with each other. When you play with your child, you reinforce their belief that you care about them and you want them to have fun. They learn that even though you may argue during the game, and even though you may compete against each other, you still care about each other. Games are a great way to promote learning at any age, and they're an invaluable tool for feeling closer to your child.

Leave a 1-Click Review!

I hope you are enjoying my book ! I would be incredibly thankful if you could take just 60 seconds to write a brief review on Amazon, even if it's just a few sentences!

>> Click here or scan the QR Code to leave a quick review

CONCLUSION

Parenting isn't always an easy job, but it's a rewarding one. The bonds we forge with our kids are strong enough to last a lifetime, especially if we reinforce them with good communication skills. Our kids may frustrate and exhaust us from time to time, but it's important to remember that kids rarely act disobedient out of pure malice. There are many adjustments we can make to our parenting styles and the ways we speak to our kids that can encourage them to be better listeners and communicators.

Throughout this book, you have learned the best strategies, tips, and secrets for effective parenting that encourages kids to listen. First, you learned the basics of child psychology, getting insight into what makes our kids tick and why they may have trouble listening to us. Next, you mentally prepared yourself and discovered how to keep frustration at bay during arguments and tantrums. Then you learned why communication is so important for kids, how listening makes them better communicators, and how you and your child can improve communication skills. Rather than reacting with anger, you now know that taking time to explain the situation to your child in terms they understand is a more productive method of conflict management. You know how to teach emotional intelligence and conversation skills to your child through fun activities and games. With all of this information, you are now ready to be the best parent you can be. Use this information to guide your child through all the hurdles of early development and prepare them for the rest of their life.

Now that you've learned how to improve communication between you and your child, all you need to do is put your newfound knowledge into practice!

Try some of the tips included in this book, keeping in mind the information you've learned about child development and the importance of remaining calm when talking to your child. Use encouraging conversation starters to get a better understanding of their feelings. Encourage them to exercise their listening skills. The more you practice the methods in this book, the stronger your bond with your child will become. You will develop mutual respect for each other, and before long you will become not just parent and child, but good friends.

If you found this book to be helpful in getting your child to listen to you, consider leaving a positive review on Amazon. This helps more parents, guardians, and teachers just like you get the help they need for establishing communication with their kids. Every parent-child relationship deserves the opportunity to flourish, and practicing good communication skills is the best way to ensure that happens for parents everywhere.

REFERENCES

AnnaliseArt. (2019, July 18). *Family in the car*. Pixabay. https://pixabay.com/illustrations/people-in-cars-family-car-4345551/

Arhavisual. (2019, June 4). *Upset child*. Pixabay. https://pixabay.com/vectors/cry-sadness-child-alone-emotions-4250450/

Cdd20. (2020, Jan. 30). *Angry thoughts*. Pixabay. https://pixabay.com/illustrations/caricature-imagination-hand-drawing-4804618/

Cherry, K. (2020, Aug. 16). *Child psychology and development*. Verywell Mind. https://www.verywellmind.com/what-is-child-psychology-2795067

CoxinhaFotos. (2017, Mar. 1). *Disobedient child.* Pixabay. https://pixabay.com/vectors/son-unemployed-parents-nervous-2106231/

GDJ. (2020, July 5). *Brain and heart.* Pixabay. https://pixabay.com/vectors/mindfulness-brain-heart-mind-body-5371476/

Headspace. (n.d.). *The science-backed benefits of meditation.* https://www.headspace.com/science/meditation-benefits

La_Petite_Femme. (2017, Sept. 17). *Elephants with balloons.* Pixabay. https://pixabay.com/illustrations/elephants-balloons-love-heart-2757831/

La_Petite_Femme. (2017, May 23). *Mom hugging her daughter.* Pixabay. https://pixabay.com/illustrations/mother-and-baby-baby-girl-mom-love-2334628/

MoteOo. (2018, Mar. 29). *Mom criticizing daughter.* Pixabay. https://pixabay.com/illustrations/mom-mum-daughter-mother-family-3273202

Shvets, A. (n.d.). *Wash your hands sign.* Pexels. https://www.pexels.com/photo/drawing-of-hands-being-washed-4226600/

Stosny, S., Ph.D. (2015, Aug. 7). *Why parents really get angry at their kids.* Psychology Today. https://www.

psychologytoday.com/intl/blog/anger-in-the-age-
entitlement/201508/why-parents-really-get-
angry-their-kids

The Communication Trust. (n.d.). *Why communication is important.* https://www.thecommunicationtrust.org.uk/media/2147/all_together_now_-_section_2.pdf

van der Linden, N. (n.d.). *8 psychologist-backed tips for improving communication with kids.* Motherly. https://www.mother.ly/child/8-expert-tips-talk-effectively-kids

Made in United States
North Haven, CT
15 February 2022